ROBERT WILSON

Robert Wilson

Franco Quadri / Franco Bertoni / Robert Stearns

Rizzoli NEW YORK

First published in the United States of America in 1998 by
RIZZOLI INTERNATIONAL PUBLICATIONS, INC.
300 Park Avenue South, New York, NY 10010

First published in Italy in 1997 by
OCTAVO Franco Cantini Editore
Borgo S. Croce 8
50122 Firenze

Copyright © 1997
OCTAVO Franco Cantini Editore

Library of Congress Cataloging-in-Publication Data

Quadri, Franco.
    [Robert Wilson. English]
    Robert Wilson / Franco Quadri, Franco Bertoni, and Robert Stearns.
            p. cm.
    Includes bibliographical references.
    ISBN 0-8478-2103-X
    1. Wilson, Robert, 1941–   –Criticism and interpretation.
2. Experimental theater. I. Bertoni, Franco. II. Stearns, Robert.
III. Title.
PN2287.W494Q2413   1998
792'.0233'092–dc21   98-110713
                                       CIP

"The Life and Times of Robert Wilson" translated and edited by Jenny McPhee
All other text translated by Richard Fremantle

Designed by Auro Lecci

Separation: Fotolito Toscana and Bluprint, Florence
Printing: Grafedit, Bergamo

Printed and bound in Italy

Contents

ROBERT WILSON

Franco Quadri

THE LIFE AND TIMES
OF ROBERT WILSON

In the beginning was time. Or was it the image? The European debut in 1971 of *Deafman Glance* at the historic Festival of Nancy introduced Robert Wilson, the new American artist responsible for relaunching representational art and restoring two-dimensional theater to Europe. At the time, the avant-garde movement was led by a concern for the expressiveness of the human body and human gestures, and their capacity to involve the audience. As always, cultural fashion was searching for what was new and controversial—the idea or style that was going to be labeled the next wave. Here was someone making himself known by relying on visual plasticity, installing a show about such simple events as the rise and fall of a theater curtain, and constructing a drama around the development of a motionless *tableau vivant* that is at the same time continuously evolving.

In *Regard du Sourd* (the show toured the continent using the French title) the references to surrealism seemed particularly apt, even though Aragon, one of the movement's leaders, deemed in his "Open letter to André Breton" (which soon became famous), such classification "as something already filed away, a subject for a thesis, for teaching, for the Sorbonne," in order to lift Wilson's show up to another level: "It is the dream of the way we once were, it is the *future* that we predicted." Wilson was, in fact, reclaiming the values of freedom: freedom from the rules of story-telling, from imposed interpretation, from conventions of recitation, but also freedom from belonging to a specific genre. And once absolved of the obligations to visual beauty, his polycentric vision of "our" hypothetical past—based in late nineteenth-century America and set in a forest out of which peers a pyramid, surrounded by improbable animals, objects plowing through the sky, and arcane geological phenomena—was free from having to correspond to one meaning.

In the shocking opening to this tragedy without catharsis, a black woman (Sheryl Sutton) kills her two small children as serenely as she fed them just a moment before. We quickly discover that we are not listening to someone narrate a story, but are instead watching the inexplicable and improbable unfolding of life, as perhaps dreamed by Raymond Andrews. He is the little deaf boy who witnesses most of what goes on from one side of the stage, letting us, the audience, see his knowing gaze as author and participant. He also lets us hear in the same debilitating way that he hears. *Deafman Glance* is "a work of silence," from which only a few remote motifs

Robert Wilson in **Deafman Glance**, 1970.

emerge every now and then in the background. The play's vocal fabric and dialogue are practically nonexistent, especially in contrast to the pronounced iron rhythm of the visual score, which shifts back and forth from acceleration to pauses, to painfully slow slow-motion, all to the beat of fast and slow time. The constant and prolonged use of "pianissimo," the interminable motionless processions that cross the stage without, however, the power to stop, the endless journey of the hand at the end of an outstretched arm as it draws towards the face, do not eliminate the presence of an "adagio" or an "andante con moto," which, with dry rhythmic contrast, acts as a verification and accentuates the atmosphere and expressive mechanisms already in place. In effect, it is the difference in the intensity of movement and the layering of different speeds inside the same image that creates an emotional release in the performance–for example, it occurs every time that, in the prevailing landscape of slow processions and rarefied gestures, a running athlete bursts onto the scene, crossing to the end of the stage, from right to left, on another wavelength, and at intervals as regular as a metronome.

Slow motion
and natural time

"In the beginning was time," we said, only to move quickly on to the image. But neither time nor the image can deny the debt owed to the psychedelic age. The fragmentation of the image is used ever more frequently in contemporary staging by directing the spectator's eye to partial close-ups of the face, or limbs or fingers, which become frozen into burning snapshots by the lights. Similarly, the fragmentation of time in *Deafman Glance* turns slow motion into one of the work's most suggestive characteristics. Time was used in much the same way as in *The Life and Times of Joseph Stalin*, following a technique already practiced by Bread and Puppet and by Richard Foreman. In Italy this technique was found in plays by Mario Ricci and Claudio Previtera, and in Japan it was adapted by the butoh dancers.

To confirm the influence of psychedelic art on Wilson's early work it is sufficient to pause for a moment to briefly describe the first and last hours of *Overture*, which in the Parisian version of 1971 lasted twenty-four hours. Both hours were lacking any action that could be called theatrical. The first rested on the emotion of the opening scene. The stage was decorated with horizontal stripes, a central geometric lake, and to the left, a golden autumnal forest of birch trees suspended in the air, revealed by an expert and intrusive play of lights. The last hour contained the gradual closing of several curtains at an unimaginably slow pace. Depicted on one curtain is the skeleton of a rampant dinosaur superimposed across the fiery crater of a burning volcano. A stag advances very slowly towards it. On both sides of the first curtain, beginning from right stage, a double, irregular proces- 11 sion of panting elderly people takes an entire hour to cross the stage; all the lights go out, except for the torch that lights up an empty throne at the center. The eyes of the dinosaur on the curtain shine; the bell tolls twelve times, and the procession continues its inexorable, invisible advance, suggesting the immobility of a painting. Testament to the infinitesimal fragmentation of space, the steps of these bearded old men cannot be heard. As in the paradox of Zeno d'Eleo, the distance between two points seems impossible to close.

Space is no longer divided into points, but into moments, and the length of the stage being crossed is equivalent to the length of an hour. The image that we see is not perceptible if it is not seen in the light of the fourth dimension. Time is presented to the audience as the key to entering into Wilson's theater through physical effort, which overcomes the passivity of mere contemplation. The abnormal length of these first performances (*Deafman Glance* is seven hours long, and is among the shortest) introduces, through prolonged gestural exhaustion, a heightened rhythm different from the rhythm of life, a rhythm of victory by means of endurance. Coupled with this rhythm in the course of the unnatural and constricting progression is the decreasing rarefaction of the rhythm of the actors, with whom, in such cases of great time expansion, whoever is watching–or better, participating–will also feel as one with regard to natural functions. I refer here particularly to sleep, which in the morning hours of *Overture* united, in an unexpected symphony, the actors lying down on the stage with the audience stretched out in their theater seats. This particular moment was important in understanding certain forms of total immersion, which is a prelude to a theatrical idea: to see a consenting spectator emerge at intervals from his own lethargy, opening his eyes every fifteen minutes in order to convince himself that nothing has changed and, from inside that heightened perception of time, noticing with emotion the insignificance of a gesture, changing colors, overlapping rhythms, and enduring the sound of a scream while suspended in a strange hypnotic dimension requiring uninterrupted and unconditional participation. But woe to anyone who breaks the spell by leaving the theater (actually the building, not just the theater hall, because the noise of the crowds in the corridors and bar are largely included in the rules of the game) to go home to take a nap, thereby crossing back into 'normality' as if it didn't matter. *Re-entering into the time of the play* becomes enormously difficult.

Wilson often challenges the 'naturalness' of time in his plays. "We are not dealing with slow motion," he once said, "but with *natural time*. The scene is aided by accelerated time, but I use the natural time that helps the sun to set, a cloud to change, a day to dawn. I allow the audience time to reflect, to meditate on other things besides those which are happening on the stage; I allow them time and space to think." But whatever definition is correct, at the bottom of this personal concept of movement there is a principle that has nothing to do with aesthetic problems. This principle involves making the actor conscious of every moment of his body's activity. For example, he is acutely aware of the act of walking in every infinitesimal phase, be it when his feet are in contact with the earth, or when his limb is precariously suspended in space, until he finally, with no chance of stopping or of accelerating, regains the millimeters that bring him back to safety. Then there is the act of bringing a cup of tea to one's lips, making a journey with one's arm, and piloting a hand intentionally and yet naturally, reacting to all the spatial implications, the environment, and the most immediate sensorial elements. As Wilson points out when he looks at a video tape of a mother picking up her crying baby from the cradle, slow motion reveals that this act of affection is interrupted, or rather, preceded by an instinctive gesture of repulsion that is invisible to the naked eye. This kind of gesture in incorporated into the *natural* movement of the actor and places the focus on his behavior rather than on his psychology. The total physicalization of the actor is reflected through his activity to the audience, which perceives the nuances of each single gesture, producing dramatic results that would otherwise be insignificant. This is similar to the effect of Warhol's early long and motionless films. It is the gesture, brought to its extreme, that then becomes the theme of the story.

Overture as a manifesto
for a new structure

*O*verture lends itself to a broader formal analysis that is decisive in its comprehension of a method and an aesthetic, given the nature of anomalous theater. It is a non-repeatable *unicum* born in the autumn of Comic Opera, taking the name but not the appearance of a springtime prelude that takes place on the four floors of the artist's home in New York City. The performance constructs an equivalent *sui generis* (twenty-four hours with seventy actors between the ages of four and seventy-two from five different parts of the world) to the summer event of 168 hours, seven days and seven nights of uninterrupted theatrical experience, aimed at the progressive climb to the top of the seven mountains that surround Persepoli. *Overture* was further enhanced by an exhibition-prologue at the Musée Galliera, which included documentation, encounters, and games, showing Wilson's pragmatic approach and study method. After the silence of *Deafman Glance* and before Wilson's real operatic explosion, sound comes out into the open in this work. On one level, sound is presented as live spoken language with broad concessions to improvisation and support from a microphone. By contrast, on a second level, sound is recorded private conversations, radio transmissions, or natural noises; and finally, a third musical tape, creating a distinct atmosphere, repeatedly plays back the same pieces.

The words of the actors never comply with narrative and rules; dialogue is never exchanged among the characters on the stage. But whether the words are meant for the audience, or whether they follow the flow and character of an inner monologue, or whether they repeat familiar passages of the text, the text takes on the role

13

Drawing by Raymond Andrews
for **KA MOUNTAIN**.

of critic by making comments, giving explanations, and providing personal narration. It also provokes or communicates immediate impressions, as in the case of Cindy Lubar, who freely abandons herself to a depressive crisis, confusing theater with reality in a scene that seems to have been constructed to undermine her. But apart from the flourishes, the words are mainly considered as elements of sound, and herein lie the derisive verbal games and the complacent and affected nonsense called new dada, much of which has risen up from the rich sources of Gertrude Stein.

The same type of simultaneous layering is also evident on the visual level. Using the magical number seven, the space is divided into several horizontal strips. Every strip is a completely autonomous, and although close in space, each event takes place a great distance from the next one in terms of time and energy. No one in these layers is part of the whole, nor does anyone look for any correlation or correspondence between the parallel spaces. The entire visual picture of seven layers is never reassembled into one, as they are in the unexpected series of superimposed images in Kenneth Anger's film. Instead, the scene is the accidental sum of a series of self-sufficient addenda that leaves the audience to choose between several images, which when assembled may recall surrealistic figures, and which with analytic scrutiny conjure up the decomposition technique of Proust. Wilson's intention is to reproduce a variety of thoughts with the speed of association and disassociation, of schizoid accumulation and fragmentation, so that the spectator, as thinking subject, must choose between the seven possibilities offered, either multiplying them or reducing them, moment by moment.

But *Overture* consists of more than a theoretical inquiry. It contains the fascination and subtle images of a story, and in addition to the emotions brought about by its visual and conceptual revelations, there is the surprise of an unexpected rediscovery. During the first hour of the work, after the complex movements of the curtains and the play of lights, we see behind the empty throne in the middle of a deserted stage, a pier running along an area of water. At extreme right stage, underneath a vertical light, the figure of an old woman enters on all fours. She moves—again unimaginably slowly—towards the far left side of the stage where she turns around and returns very slowly to the curtain where she first appeared. Suddenly she stands up and, again walking with the same slow, elusive rhythm, she goes to the end of the pier, approaches an empty chair, and sits down. She makes a quick gesture, and stands up. We hear a frivolous melody from the loudspeakers. She says something unintelligible. She makes another gesture aimed out beyond the sea. Then darkness. The tolling of a bell tells us that one hour has gone by. Except for the theater staff, no one recognizes the woman walking on all fours—who will remain motionless on the stage, seated in the shadows, for at least another hour—as Madeleine Renaud in a cameo performance.

The participation of the French actress, who is over seventy years old, is perhaps today less extraordinary than it used to be, but it is significant for the contradiction it presents. On one hand it is a show of modesty, of education and faith in the value of perennial research (and in the personality of whoever proposes it). On the other hand it is the researcher's tribute to tradition, and one of the first important ways in which Wilson involves the audience with a great performer—something he will do consistently in his work, and not only in terms of actors on the stage. The cameo performance is secondary to his desire to include famous artistic personalities in his "family," which constitutes the basis of Wilson's work, and which will always accompany him as he broadens and renews performances for international audiences.

The family on top of the seven holy mountains of Shiraz

The "family," at first, consisted of his own relatives, members and intellectual bureaucrats from the society of artists, the Byrd Hoffman School of Byrds, and producers and agents dressed up as fans. Other people absolutely essential to him were Bénedicte Pesle and the legendary Ninon Talon Karlweis, who was set on fire once by the Japanese of Terayama during a show, and who nearly died while accompanying Wilson on tour. She was as much a visionary spectator as her protégé, Wilson. She was an elderly talent scout who was unable to remain

The $ Value of Man, 1975.

awake once she took her seat in the theater, but afterwards she was capable of narrating every detail of the performance, which she assimilated while she was asleep. But the family is mostly made up of Wilson's favorite students, who have graduated from a school of disabled actors where Wilson used to teach, and which originally gave Wilson a reason to continue his work. Raymond Andrews was the deaf mute in *Glance*, Cindy Lubar risked schizoid disassociation in *Overture*, and Christopher Knowles used his uncoordinated movements and stuttering in *A Letter for Queen Victoria*. With even greater freedom and autonomy in *Einstein on the Beach*, the actors simultaneously played subjects and objects in performances for which they were both co-authors and audience.

The family was at the center of the performance created for the Festival of Shiraz in 1972, entitled KA MOUNTAIN AND GUARDenia TERRACE: "a story about a family and some people changing," which became the introduction to *Overture*, and was a marathon of a terrifying duration and number of performers. It told of a tribal event, and included a zoo of real and make-believe animals, among which is the ever-present dinosaur. The actors' exercises and mediations become part of an unending series of pieces, performed consecutively and in contrast to the display of references to both Eastern and Western symbols and archetypes, taking as much time as the Creation. The action occurs during the ascent of the mountain called Halt Tanan (Seven Bodies), named for seven martyred sufi. (This recalls passages from *Deafman Glance*, especially the opening sacrifice.) The Three Magi, Othello, Merlin the magician, and Saint Theresa of Avila, appear in scenes of the Apocalypse and Disneyland. All arrive at the top of the mountain on the seventh day, "after having lived the entire history of humanity and every one of our most secret compulsions." Unfortunately we will never really know what happened because what remains of this event is the misled and confused information reported by newspapers at the time, together with some photos from the family album.

Robert Wilson and Christopher Knowles in **Dia log/Network**, Florence 1977.

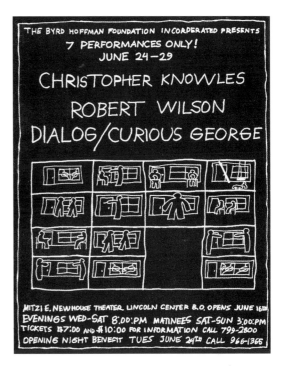

Poster by Christopher Knowles for **Dialog/Curious George**,
New York 1980.

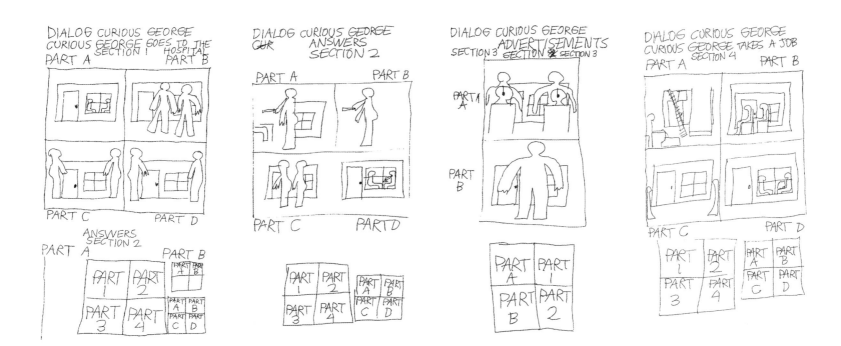

Drawings by Christopher Knowles for the four sections of **Dialog/Curious George**.

Two dramatic moments, however, can be extracted from the epic and Wilson's basic theme. One of the short pieces, *Jail*, was dedicated to the days Wilson spent in a prison in Cyprus, right before the Festival, for possession of hashish. An enormous figure is seen scratching his chest for four hours on top of a pile of rubble. The scene of Wilson's arrest follows, and the attempt of two of his friends (Ann Wilson and Cindy Lubar) to visit him in prison. The same movement and the same dialogue with the police are repeated forty-seven times: "May we see our friend?" "L.S.D., no," "Oh! (long pause) Whatever will become of us?" The second moment concerned the death sentence of an Iranian student, Mehdi Reza, against which the theater company presented a vain appeal on the day before the final performance. Wilson turned up at the last press conference with a blindfold over his eyes as if before an execution squad.

The performance:
solos and duets with Chris Knowles

Although people in the news sometimes appear in Wilson's plays–for example, Wilson himself in *Jail* and Patricia Hearst in *Einstein on the Beach*–his performance style remains rigorously abstract, with the only reality being that of self-expression. Between 1974 and 1980, solo performances seemed like introductions to the artist, evenings that recaptured and isolated moments from more important plays, beginning with the opening scene of *Deafman Glance*, which is by now emblematic of Wilson's body of work. Sometimes these moments were shown on video, but more often they were an opportunity for Wilson to freely express himself through both verbal and psycho-physical exercises. In the first instance, he used verbal acceleration and assonance, and in the second, he employed the dynamic techniques of yelling and dancing, in a kind of physical training session enhanced by writing and by symbols on the walls or on pieces of stretched cloth. The most joyful moments, however, occurred in the duets with Chris Knowles, for the most part based on repetition, with Wilson in the role of stimulator or supporter. Knowles, who revealed his poetic talent by writing some scenes for *Einstein,* and much more recently for *T.S.E.*, is also co-author of *The $ Value of Man*, which begins with the reading of a newspaper, but soon involves scenic structures and dance numbers. He also worked on various editions of *Dia Log* (among them *Dia Log/Network* and *DiaLog/Curious George*), which is an exhilarating and obsessive parody of television, playing on reiteration and disassociation. In this piece, vocal exchange or dialogue is often substituted by confrontation with sound, with the possible variant of Chris's stuttering and his inexpressive and abstract repetition of meanings. A tape recorder or video camera is insistently used as another interlocutor, and for the continuous salvaging of passages that have just been read.

A Letter for Queen Victoria.
The montage letter to the Queen
from the show program.

On all levels, the Wilsonian actor does not so much portray the consciousness of the character he is play-ing, because, through the emphasis placed on the freedom of his body and through the encouragement of his impulses, his own subconscious is revealed. Within an imposed structure over which he has no control what-soever, the actor is confronted with the problem of acting "naturally," even if his gestures are directed, and even if at times he has to limit himself to repeating exercises already assimilated, but to be lived over again autonomously in the present. If in the general picture he finds himself acting as an instrument, his mode of intervention cannot be instrumental. The immediacy of his action will not come so much from his ability to demonstrate his own internal rhythm, as from a network of sensitive contacts established with his companions, which allows him to enter into synthesis with them. In the final analysis, this is theater that tends to establish physiopsychic relationships among the actors, and of course the origins of this can be found in the therapeutic applications of its beginnings.

From Lloyd to Glass:
many ways to write an opera

In this climate of experimentation and fragmentation, *A Letter for Queen Victoria* seems like a pause meant to be a formal reassurance, directed towards the historical lie that permits beautiful, upper-class, slightly operatic cos-tumes, like those we see on opening night at Spoleto. In fact, the schematic organization of the space used in pre-ceding works is put aside somewhere, although the conceptual precedent that begins with the image remains

19

Einstein on the Beach, 1976.
Sheryl Sutton and Lucinda Childs
in the second *knee play*.

operative. But the dimension of sound, which incorporates even the words, in the sense of infusing them into the fabric of continuous singing, adds another layer to the preceding work.

In the prologue an informal letter is read, as indicated by the title, but over the following four acts, which are deliberately unequal in length, a storyline is never developed. In the second act familiar rhythms are incessantly repeated and suggest a temporal dissection, while a group of air force men occupy a fragmented reality, destined to renew itself like the time machine in *Morel's Invention*; the third act is a striking evocation of another era with a frenetic, but paradoxically, an almost whispered dance of hands on small tables in a Victorian cafe. The first and fourth acts are more interesting in terms of their relation to each other, and contain an admirable contrast of figures–for example, the white woman and the black woman–and narrative intrusions that seems a bit forced, to signal transitions. The piece is dominated by black and white, the antithesis of time, and unequal acts. It introduces the not-entirely-speculative theme of doubles, and unfolds along oblique lines instead of along the usual multiplicity of horizontal lines. The climax in the first and fourth acts consists of a sharp and modulated scream that is continued on a single note to the limits of all possible resistance. The voice becomes an instrument, and the sound elevates gradually, above the mannerist, Schubert-like score of Alan Lloyd. The singers remain in the orchestra pit and do not enter directly onto the stage. The music is part of the sound, just like the tape in *Overture*, though this time the work expressly requires such accompaniment, and because the music is live and not on tape, it remains in the foreground. Dialogue also makes a timid appearance, but can barely be heard and seems to have little overall significance.

Queen Victoria, however, is not yet an opera in the same sense as *Einstein on the Beach*. The music by Philip Glass, obsessively repeating its few notes–a river that for almost five hours is the supporting element in the undivided whole of a composition where scenic action and musical score seem to unite so perfectly that it is impossible to tell which element comes first. Following the "theatre-as-image," is it now possible to talk of a "theater-as-sound?" In reality the invasion of the music completely conditions the rhythm of the action, and not only is the rhythm conditioned, but Wilson is stimulated, whenever possible, to work *against* the action. But it is not possible, because Glass's music is all-inclusive, and the endless series of numbers–"one two three one two three"– that is sung is not enough to express Einstein and his theories, since the words devour the universe from which they come. *Einstein* is precisely anti-*Deafman Glance* because of the way in which absolute sound substitutes everything and continues with great effect until all resonance disappears. Fullness replaces emptiness with a wall as thick as the wall built around Raymond Andrews. Wilson even complained later about the effect the wall of deafness had on the interactions among the actors on stage.

A train, a courthouse, a field, and a time machine

And what if the staging were enough to express *Einstein*? Beyond the objections to the score from a musical point of view, and beyond also the enthusiastic reactions that were provoked by the masterpiece at its debut in 1976, time also intervened in Wilson's favor with a series of revivals. The revivals were a miracle for a colossus such as *Einstein*, today so problematic to stage, and it even enjoyed a spectacular European tour. In order to further analyze the piece, it is useful to look at its conceptual origins. Let us start with the genre of "biography," which Wilson, as a good American, favors and theatrically cultivates. Perhaps, however, biography is simply a pretext, a way to access personal meaning given the parameters of Wilson's art, which preclude story-telling. This is exemplified by two works *nominally* dedicated to Freud and Stalin, which are in reality much less biographical than the works written for Raymond Andrews or Cindy Lubar, two leading actors close to the playwright but not famous. The premise for *Einstein*, however, makes one think of the letter in *Queen Victoria*. As the title suggests, the idea for the play was born at the suggestion of an old photograph, taken in 1905, of the scientist on the beach, which is projected for the audience at a certain point in the show.

The leading criterion for the composition of the work, staged thanks to the co-production of five festivals, is not that it tell a story, nor that it be logical, but that it comply with simple figurative associations, according to a technique that is in some way mathematical. Three images, combining interiors and exteriors, were chosen–a train inserted in a vacant quadrilateral space, a symmetrical courthouse with surreal elements, an uncultivated field. We return to each of these images three times, and each time the image is approached from a different angle, playing on a succession of different pictorial planes, which influences the arrangement of the actors on stage, who each time take on the form of a *portrait*, a *still life*, or a *landscape*. For example, at the beginning the train appears to be advancing from right to left at the rear of the stage, while the second time we see the end of the train in the foreground as it slowly departs from a station. The courthouse, first seen from the front during a trial in which Einstein (Lucinda Childs) is a defendant, is sectioned off in such a way that when we see it again the right half has become a prison where Einstein is being held. Einstein is transformed into Patricia Hearst (the daughter of the king of journalism, who became an armed feminist and a heroine of the newspapers of the day). The field is visited by an aircraft hovering in space, which, the second time we see it, seems noticeably larger because of its closeness. The third time around, each of the three elements is transfigured: the train becomes the facade of a building of which we see the outline; the courthouse is now the prison bed, standing vertical and illuminated on one side, and essentially becoming a strip of lights as it very slowly ascends into the sky. The exterior of the field becomes the interior of the spaceship (or more precisely, the "time machine") already floating in the air.

The opera was written with visual rhythm, and concentrates on the relationship between the characters and the area they occupy. The four acts without intermission are separated by between-act punctual little junctures, or "*knee plays*," performed in front of the curtain and orchestrated by two women (Lucinda Childs and Sheryl Sutton), fittingly dressed as travelers from outer space, and representative of the unstable equilibrium to which they are both subjected. The time warp is in keeping with the repetition of the same few notes by Glass, which rise undaunted from voices in the orchestra pit in a litany of three notes, or of three numbers, always the same, one two three, one two three, one two three. The sound reiterates the obsession with numbers that has already determined the movement of the scenes, and restates the dominant themes of equilibrium and solemnity, of heavy gestures in a cluttered geometry. During his years working with Wilson, the choreographer Andy De Groat persisted, in the name of freedom, towards an appropriation of the body in which everyone becomes part of the infinitely rotating sphere: an infinite circle, fast or slow, diligently drawn from the inspiration of a flying dervish or Indian reflection, like learning to walk again, in an amazingly sensitized and concentrated system, the entire body concentrating, listening, in order to absorb the sense of movement from every vibration. The plot of *Einstein,* which seems to concentrate on the relationship between the actor and the stage, appears almost scientifically determined: first in the contrast of gesture and rhythm and the near absence of scenic accessories; second in the oppression of the stage set on a choir that is only described objectively; and finally in the conquest of the scenic space, which corresponds to the new awareness of the body. The lighting is, of course, not extraneous (and emphasizes geometric elements and the discovery of various scenic depths), which contributes to the determination of different temporal zones in scenes which take place at various times during the day. Significantly, the opening of space and the burst of light provide a passage into the spectator's sensibility, coinciding finally in a moment of freedom for all who watch.

Einstein on the Beach. Scene plan by Robert Wilson.

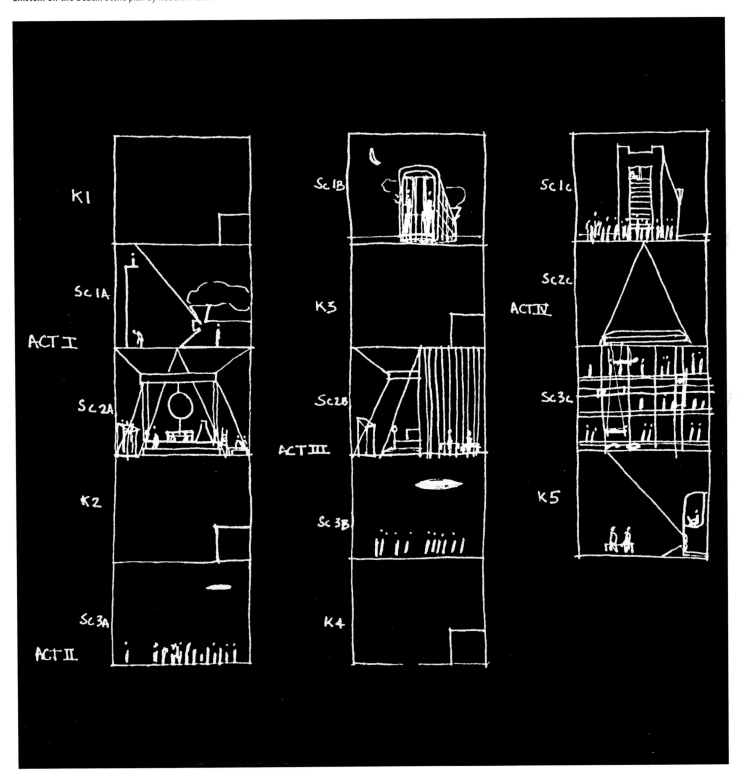

Robert Wilson and Philip Glass.

The result is the great
American opera

The magic moment of the big scene of the apotheosis is similar to a story by Borges or a story from the Chassidim unveiling the word that means God. Wilson arrives at the pinnacle of his achievement, the music reaches its fullest range, and Glass writes his *Hymn to Joy*. It is the scene for which *Einstein* was conceived, with all the triumph of a big musical finish. The spaceship finally lands, opening its doors to the audience. Fifteen actors appear, their backs to the spectators and each enclosed in a square compartment. They play different instruments simultaneously while making symmetrical gestures and contrasting movements, and maneuver a set of lights so as to illuminate the back of the stage and the oblique or circular lines that direct and animate the movements of the work. While a man flies across the space, these lines determine, in depth and in height, horizontally and vertically, the trajectory of two flying pendulums, suspended like two swings in the void, and functioning as both human containers and symbols of time. A hammering, fragmented sound signals to us the impending event, and is paralleled by equally insistent and prolonged gestures. Sound, space, and time: the climax expands the known and not-so-well-known dimensions.

Beyond the constant molecular breaking up of reality, as suggested by the musical language, references to Einstein are scattered throughout the evening, from the violinist in the front line of the orchestra whose features resemble those of Einstein as an old man, to all the actors who identify with him, to the series of projected photographs of him, to the gyroscope that is slowly lowered by a string hanging from the ceiling in honor of a beloved toy that once belonged to the scientist as a child. But the ghost of his thought emerges more sharply in the crossing of the fundamental problem of space with equally crucial problems of time in the theater. By bringing the phantom of the

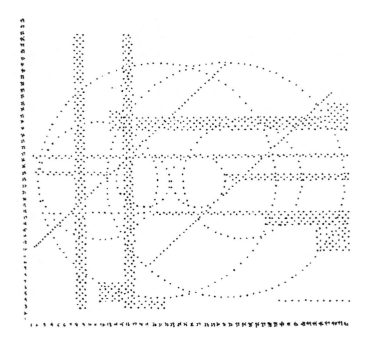

A diagram of the movements,
drawn by Lucinda Childs, for the third
knee play and scene 3c, act IV of
Einstein on the Beach.

Einstein on the Beach, 1976. The interior of the 'time machine' in act IV.

25

scientist on to his own turf, Wilson succeeds in internalizing him, recognizing many of the same questions he asked as he formed his own artistic expression, which led to the discovery of a language, which constitutes the climax of the opera. Inside the time (and space) machine are hidden and revealed not mathematical calculations, but the lines of upholding the opera–as precise a deciphering of his art as the author will allow. Behind his studied choreography, and the musical explosion of Glass, appears the abstract geometry of Busby Berkeley, the luxuriant corporeal axioms of the Ziegfield Follies. From outerspace, the time machine has brought us the new musical.

By 1976 the formalistic ideal of the "big American musical" was visible at the end of the long corridor of Wilson's dreams. I intend to talk about individual shows, but first I would like to allude to the musical model written by those composers of by-now classic grandeur, which today might be unthinkable for anyone besides our utopian Texan. According to Wilson, these composers should be required to collaborate with the spiritual and sublime purity of the idol Balanchine. American culture, which attracts European audiences to Wilson, has from the beginning formed Wilson's expanding eye, and pushed him to create through the use of capricious and irresistibly immediate images according to a principle of association (and disassociation). We recall in this regard his 1978 video, *Video50*, which presents one hundred striking mini-dramas one after another, each unrelated, and each lasting thirty seconds, bringing about a kind of bombardment of the eye, with instantaneous movements within moments from everyday life, objects, people. The video captures and expresses the reality of our advertising-age, blink-of-an-eye attention span, and should be placed, according to the author, over escalators in department stores, on juke boxes, in subways, wherever by now, not even twenty years later, the "real" version of this visual nightmare has succeeded in reaching us. But the quality of Wilson's image sends us back to the culture of American life which emerges often in his work, from the stage settings, to the deep South of the autobiographical *Deafman Glance*, to the task for biography in *Einstein*. This cultural heritage also dictates the optimistic epilogue of the show, like the happy ending of a movie–a final measured and banal conversation between two people in praise of the quiet life. For the first time, however, in a preceding sequence the same work brought up national events with a brief almost heroic apparition of Patricia Hearst, taken directly from a famous photograph in a magazine.

Einstein the defendant,
Hearst the terrorist

In the first scene of the third act, a peculiar courtroom is invaded by a partially assembled bed so that, left stage, only half of the bed is seen next to a judge's bench on the left, while on the right, iron bars descend from the ceiling, forming a prison around two prisoners, its back wall cracked and chipped away. Suddenly we see Childs, until then dressed as Einstein the defendant, change into a debutante in a white gown (Patricia Hearst) standing in front of the prison, together with a companion, his jacket around her shoulders. She bends down, and when she rises she is wearing trousers and holding a machine gun; the jacket is gone and she is dressed all in black. She turns towards the audience and we see that she is wearing handcuffs. One of the prisoners imitates many of her gestures. With dry precision, the actress-dancer subsequently assumes an astonishing procession of poses (and relative costumes) based on a series of newspaper photographs, expressing no dramatic component nor any rhythmic connection between stances. After she leaves, the entire scene is repeated, gesture by gesture, breath by breath, in the same identical place, by Sheryl Sutton, who, in contrast to Childs, is dressed in white—a perfect photographic negative of the first Patricia Hearst. In the sense of return and reversal of this captivating moment, in the pale echo of the just-lived reality represented by a prisoner's bed descending from the ceiling and a defendant's chair already on the stage, but now seen in miniature, far away, faded into memory, lies another key to a play that takes on the theme of space and its relation to time.

Almost immediately, we see Childs seated at the back of the stage, behind a crack in the wall of her cell. After her actions have been copied and erased, she no longer exists as a character, but as a distant part of one memory and, in fact, only spied off stage through a narrow opening. The girl dressed in all white sits on a white chair in a white space under a white light. Aside from the double square in the right foreground where the knee plays occur, this whiteness is the only island in the gray of the play (according to legend, ninety-nine different tonalities of gray and beige, all taken from Magritte's palette). And the sparkling light that floods Childs—who is virtually off stage—is the only visible source, after the parallel and horizontal stripes in the background have been extinguished. All the other scenic props are also slowly disassembled while Childs remains alone on stage. The theater is decomposed and is exposed without pity, while Lucinda launches into a long tirade by Christopher Knowles that consists of his sensitive summary of *Einstein*, written after a rehearsal. Again the play folds in on itself and even the back-drop disappears.

A man and a woman, two doubles

A short piece entitled *I Was Sitting On My Patio This Guy Appeared I Thought I Was Hallucinating* followed *Einstein* after almost a year, at the Cherry Lane Theatre in New York, before then entering the official international circuit. A man and a woman, Bob Wilson and Lucinda Childs, each perform alone, one after the other, for forty minutes. The two acts are separated by darkness. Both actors say the same things (more or less), each using the

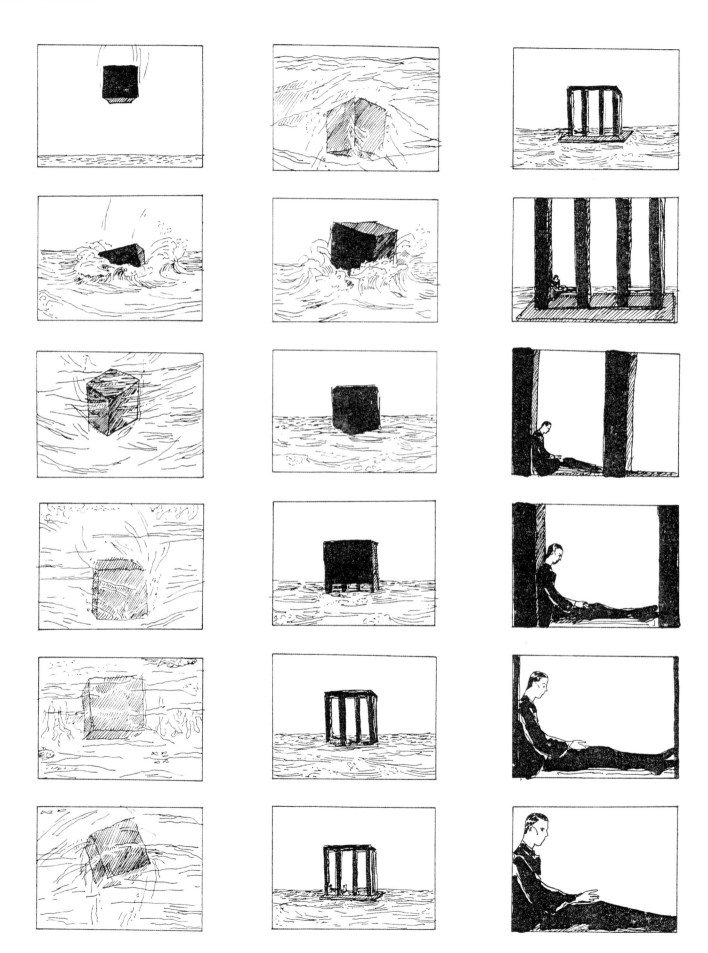

I Was Sitting On My Patio…, 1977.
Parallel sequences from the TV
storyboard by Thomas Woodruff.

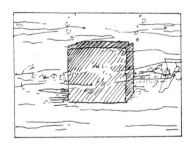

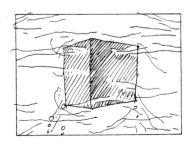

29

same gestures (except for some nuances). Meanwhile, in the same ascetic space, which is literally polished to a shining finish, among the signature geometries and sparse rigid furniture, in front of lit arches or a dark bookcase, small screens descend, showing little insignificant commercials or short films predominantly about animals, penguins for him, ducks for her, against the sound of light harpsichord and piano music by Lloyd, and the intermittent interruption of a man's voice. The process repeats the double female pantomime of *Einstein* just described, but there is a more pertinent precedent in *Dia Log*, in which Wilson and Knowles used the same diagrammed space to copy or counter each other's respective actions. Wilson's canon of repetition suggests the human capacity to act as a human on any given day, in the spirit of Beckett in the second *Act without words*; and what are interesting, as suggested and reinforced by the stage set, are precisely the tiny variations found in the repetitive movements.

In some ways, what we are witnessing is a study of the body's mechanical movements–movements that are memorized by our muscles, as in the case, for example, of a classical ballet dancer. For him, in particular, such mechanical gestures ultimately rely upon the straight line, as does the set design, all within a fragmented structure, the pieces of which all correspond and are multiples of each other: four minutes, thirty-two minutes, etcetera. The overall effect is not unlike the sensation of wandering through the ineffable architectural harmony of an antique Japanese garden. In this script, one of the first written by Wilson for the theater, music, lights, and gestures are kept separate from the recitation and independent from the text, but the piece is still far from the smoothness found in *Edison* or the rhythm of *Die Goldenen Fenster* (*The Golden Windows*), both of which are capable of making sense out of a fabric of nonsense. Here the re-cycling operation still naively makes us feel Wilson's desire to be casual, reflecting, according to the author himself, more on our way of thinking than on the way in which we normally speak, almost as if our head were a television set that moves from thought to thought in the same way one changes channels. But the result is embarrassing. The attempt to construct a collage made up of bits of plot, false memories, and banal conversations, mixed with psychological absurdities and sociological contortions, in an Albee-like fashion, empties the behavioral action of all meaning and reduces it to a purely demonstrative piece of information. Deprived of supporting structures, the polished perfection of the environment leans even more towards a reading of the play as a mannerist salvaging of Broadway. It is too soon to determine whether this could instead be seen as a prelude to the director's future scenographic standards, when under the threat of the serialization of his work, he may succumb to becoming a "genre" of his own.

Death Destruction and
Detroit, 1979. Prologue.

A return to revival
for a secret biography

The subsequent *Death Destruction and Detroit*, more familiarly known as *D.D.& D.*, sanctions a return to the past, while marking Wilson's debut in the German Federal Republic, which is destined to become his economic homeland as he finds work there for the entire decade of the 1980s and beyond. Perhaps he left his heart and his prestige behind in Paris, the city which he adopted in 1971, and which still reserves a place for him every year at the Festival d'Automne. Before a new audience, like the one in Berlin, a bit disarmed by certain leaps of logic and ready to hide behind hilarity, Wilson works with Schaubühne in her scenographic laboratory, constructing the endless plots drawn in black and white on backdrops. And from the dressmakers he pillages hundreds of costumes, all of which have in common the familiar thread of expressionism mixed with the severity of Leni Riefenstahl. In this environment, Bob finds the occasion for a retrospective of his work in a monumental five-hour performance in which, together with some striking previously-unpublished pieces, he pours out all the Wilsonism of the past. For his new homeland, however, it is all new: the rhythm is slow, time is extenuated, there is an indication of impending disaster, flying saucers return in the form of airborne racing cars informing the title of the performance, and there is a comparison of eras, from the exploration of the moon to prehistoric animals.

But the climax of the evening, which has effectively renewed ancient emotions without relying on memory, is the very long scene, divided into three sections, that opens the second part of the work. Behind a small child in the foreground dressed in a red Napoleon costume, there is a group of couples wearing black evening clothes who are dancing on the darkened stage in white profile, while diagonal light bursts from a series of opened doors studding the backdrop. From these doors, a quintet of symmetrical waiters make repeated entrances in order to serve a symmetrical meal as in a big musical. The dancing couples then transform into clusters of isolated fig-

31

ures, motionless, leaving only one character, an old man (a Nazi) to weave in and out among them, spiraling in an endless dance, drawn out over more than an hour like the festival of Dionysus in the Living Theatre's production of *Antigone*. His dance is suspended between the nostalgia of a lost waltz and the aimless turning that was a leitmotif in the grand vision of early Wilson, and expresses Busby Berkeley fantasies, in much the same manner as the ending of *Einstein on the Beach*. Mistrusting ideology, the director is content with the revival, just like a time not long before when he experimented with the verbal games of Gertrude Stein (which he continues to do). Here he seems to want to depict the world of the intellectual refugee, placing impeccable German actors in an atmosphere of Parisian *haute couture* of the 1930s, among the white-clad ghosts of spent lives like those found in F. Scott Fitzgerald, dressed with their problems of boredom and wealth.

But behind this formal elegance that enchanted critics and visitors from all over Europe—apart from my own affectionate shadow of a doubt due to an aestheticism that seemed to want to replace ideology and fed on an exaggerated accumulation of citations from his own work and style—this "opera with music in two acts" or "love story in sixteen scenes" contained a new imaginary biography, which was, however, unacknowledged by the theater management because it was dedicated to Rudolph Hess, a Nazi criminal still incarcerated in Berlin's Spandau prison at the time of the Berlin performance, as well as to Albert Speer, architect and theorist of the Nazi regime. Simple description and objective commentary, without making any judgment, provide occasional traces leading to Hess and contribute to the piece one of its major threads (I don't dare call it the plot). Wilson was impressed by this strange man, for the bizarre things he did as well as for the poetic letters he wrote to Hitler: a man who after almost forty years of isolation inside a prison cell still remained faithful to Nazism, a man who at Nuremberg refused to hire a defense lawyer, never repenting his decision, a man by now completely insane, incarcerated under the control of 380 people placed in three four-story buildings, at a cost to the four allied powers of half a million dollars a year. What first interested the director was Hess's insanity, an interest originally captured by the American monster, David "son of Sam" Berkowitz: a serial killer of women, who refused to claim the insanity defense and was sentenced to more than five hundred years in prison, to be spent entirely under the terrifying eye of closed-circuit television, which watched him and recorded his every gesture, twenty-four hours a day. According to the author, "the subject was woven into the piece like a thread in a carpet," and these contaminations, often typically American, will continue to crop up in his work. "The whole performance is about Hess," Wilson confirms, "and a large part of it is made up of words actually spoken by the Nazi leader." It is strange that no German critic noticed, or perhaps they repressed it, since all the actors were aware of Hess's role. Even two actresses who had been in a camp during the war did not share the official prejudice against "the naive American," who neglected his intellectual responsibility. Paradoxically, the clandestine and undeclared biography was much less evasive and contained more information than the readily available biographies.

In the apocalyptic atmosphere of *D.D.& D.*, Wilson peeks back at the 1930s and science fiction moon landings (also the responsibility of Hess) and tells a love story about two young Aryans, against a scenery of bourgeois living rooms, the cab of a bus, schematic panoramas, brick walls, streets filled with long, slow processions, a huge rock in the sea, a black crater, a hyperreal couple laying in the sun, a surreal aviator, a plunge into a color postcard of Miami, an enormous nightmarish elephant trunk, and two dinosaurs with very small brains and sharp teeth who are locked in battle..

Inside the theater
of memory

Other concepts besides biography also suggest an imaginary chronicle of events closely tied to the fable. The duplicity of *Patio*, for example, creates a similar effect. In *Patio* scenes in the second half repeat those already seen in the first, each time subtracting or adding elements, in a game of outside and inside, of full and empty, while the characters are reflections of each other in much the same way as the black and white girls in both *Queen Victoria* and *Einstein*. The dialogue is more studied compared to *D.D.& D.*, although the unaccustomed audience will still be stunned by the inconsequential dialogue. The endless and vacuous German words become dramatic not because of their non-existent significance, but because of their non-existence itself, and because the pronunciation of the words in a range of highs and lows, in guttural and sweet sounds, echo a language that was preeminently that of the musicians. This against a background of instrumental music by Lloyd, often faint and remote, but filled in, for example, with inserts by Jarrett.

It is useful for an author to rethink a work that has been written seventeen years ago, but it can also be useful for an audience to try to find new ways to understand it. After all, through the flash of images created or salvaged in order to then cancel each other out, Wilson produces a theater of memories, and it is nice to be able to go back, after some time has passed, to our recollections, when it is no longer possible to compare ourselves to the shadows in the caves. I can go back over *D.D.& D.* and unexpectedly see it differently now. I see it in the form of a Gothic journey in gray, often colored black, or suddenly white when lit by electric current–the famous, never-to-be-forgotten giant lightbulb behind which Otto Sander, but I should say Hess, hides, or maybe he actually comes into focus as the two sides of the lightbulb create the effect of a magnifying glass.

If in *Edison* we find once again the tiresome taste for the visual perfection of Strehler (who hosted *Patio* at the Piccolo Teatro), Wilson's motivations are in complete contrast to Strehler's. He refuses all psychological and aesthetic explanations of his work, and for the same reason rejects texts that are not his own and that might

33

impose upon him subject matter that is different from the form. Thus the appearance on stage of Edison, after Freud, Stalin, Queen Victoria, Einstein, and Hess, who still has not confessed, accompanied by LaFayette, Washington, Ford, Westinghouse, and other less-famous builders of the American miracle, responds to the absolute necessity of filling the abstract music with a structure all its own, with a "subject" and a pretense of action. Then, proceeding from the "biographical" series to the voices of "inventors," why not aim for the hagiography of the United States, concentrating on those Americans who made the epic story of their country even greater because they are self-made and at the same time children of consumerism? Moreover, it is the one-hundredth anniversary of the invention of the lightbulb.

A postcard
from the Statue of Liberty

It is not without irony that Wilson chooses to work on a commemorative piece reminiscent of a school pageant. The show is organized around a maniacal collection of anecdotal detail taken from the life of the leading character. Between the opening with Lafayette, official spokesperson for the Declaration of Rights (the incentive that pushes the inventor's parents to emigrate to America), and the fireman's death scene at the end, in which his last words ("Go ahead, America...") cause the Statue of Liberty to go dark, almost everything concerns the life of this patent specialist. He is dressed in a white suit and indifferently played by various actors. His two wives are beside him. Fragments of dialogue attributed to him are repeated in changing contexts, a recording of his real voice is heard, and the between-acts display enlargements of stupendous photographs of him, then there is his accident with a locomotive, and a fatal pistol shot. Included, of course, are also his inventions with their relative applications: the lightbulb screwed in and lit by a worker, a blue picture similar to Klein that reproduces liquid electricity, the phonograph, the telegraph, and the movie projector, which shows us an authentic boxing scene in a still frame from the end of the century, duplicated live by two boxers in slow motion, just like in an old show by Mario Ricci. Nor are we spared his glories, from the newly electrified foyer of the Paris Opera with its "ridiculous" chandeliers to the newly erected Statue of Liberty with its artificially lit torch. But once these pedantic elements have been introduced, Wilson deliberately denies them a recognizable human context: the two wives who alternate with each other on stage, a white woman and a black woman, function only as universalized or limited representations of their chromatic difference; and the tawny brown laboratory over the course of the show is transformed into four different interior reconstructions, and makes us wonder to what end. Are these transformations important in aid of themselves, or are they important to the workers who change the scenery, or important for the atmosphere of liberation they create, or important for their simple numerical combination?

Every temptation to impose a literary interpretation is also denied, as the text resembles rather a musical score also touching on various themes, each of which corresponds to a color. The significance of the image arises once more. In the domain of the visual, the equivalent of biography is found in the collection of postcards, and Wilson's postcard searches for its pictorial influences. In the first and fourth acts of *Edison*, the mark of Hopper and the charm of Hockney's 1950s are clearly operative, and in the second act we are taken further back to Ben Shan, while the third act is itself a postcard summed up in the stroke of a lightswitch at the Opera. Beginning in the second act, out gushes the America of yesteryear, of Southern white neoclassic houses with lawns, which we have seen before in Wilson's early work. But here, this tormented country of the past, represented by the persistent immobility of the people on stage who appear to be elements in a painting that are constantly being reshuffled, comes up against technology. It is not so much the affectionately paleoindustrial subject matter of this act and its wealth of para-scientific details that impress, but rather the extensive technical research which forms the basis for the show.

Light, sound, and action:
when the plot is the structure

Let's take lights, for example. One is struck by the recourse to particular constants (a window in a house that is always lit, lampshades in a laboratory that are always on), but it is the variants that escape us, the different gradations of luminosity on different areas of the stage. For a face or a hand to stand out with all possible *chiaroscuro*, six different electric sources are needed. And as for sound, eleven tracks are used, as in Altman's *Nashville*. On one we hear Scarlatti, on another a cantata by grasshoppers, then some electronic vibrations, an incidental conversation, a deliberately awkward whistle, together with the voices of the actors on stage, amplified by microphones but stereophonically directed by their respective echoes. The score of *Edison* is based on the discordant coupling of light and sound, with the insertion of a double line-up of actors who move and walk in time, counting the steps and rhythms of every gesture, before going back to stand immobile in places determined by sound and light. There is not only no attempt to harmonize the visual with the additive layering, the aim is towards their divergence and against all traditional values of comprehension.

Once again Wilson works with dissociation. Before *Edison*, in his imagination there was an image, a sound, an idea for a structure: four acts like those in *Queen Victoria*, the third act again very brief, two external acts that enclose two internal acts; the first one takes place at night and the last act during the day, with the dark laboratory and the Opera Garnier all lit up in the center–two *warm* acts and two *cold* acts and an obsession with sound comparable only to his visual obsession. In order to achieve a symmetrical composition, the movements and the words of the first act are repeated in the fourth act, always with only a few characters on stage, for brief sequences separated by darkness and then immediately regenerated by light. The characters, however, suddenly change, and all that is left are gestures and words against a background of a house, which presents first its facade and then its side, during a long but impressive period of time.

In the end nothing should be left but an abstract composition, like a painting or a piece of music. It becomes a work of only signs, splendidly polished in tribute to Broadway or the grand old Hollywood, a recovery in outline of the *American musical*. Beyond its visual pleasures, given the clarity of its theoretical position, *Edison* is as important to the understanding of the basis of Wilson's work as *Overture*.

At the time of the production, I collected a few statements from the artist: "I believe first of all in informal theater. I already said that the character of Edison interested me less than the character of Hess, but it is important to reaffirm that in any case for me structure comes before plot. In *Edison* the plot is in the relationship between light and darkness, between sound and silence." "My texts are not meant to tell a story, they are constructed like actual musical scores. All the gestures of the characters are numbered, all the rhythms of the lights and of the actions are calculated to the second, as in a score in which light, sound, and action converge." "*Edison* was not conceived from a story but from a structure, and from the observation that for everyone there exists the possibility of seeing and hearing both simultaneously and independently. While you speak you can listen, and while you watch one thing you can hear another. The show is above all an attempt to push as far as possible the discrepancy between image and hearing. And thus between light and sound."

A text and a plan for an apocalyptic warning:
Die Goldenen Fenster

It will not be long before the productions put on in the new German state theaters become *de rigeuer*. This will also determine the production's gradual conversion into a theater of prose, for which Wilson, at least for now, insists on making the rules, in the sense that he himself continues as the author who, with the complicity of the translators, gives a material character to the words, including sound and visual information capable of shaping the actors' performance. *Die Goldenen Fenster* (*The Golden Windows*), inspired by the American fable of the same title, was written in 1982 and produced the same year at the Kammerspiele in Munich. The text was assigned to traditional actors of great renown such as Peter Luhr and Maria Nicklisch (who were at their peak as Otto Sander in *D.D.& D.*, roles they accepted out of curiosity and a desire for a new experience) and reveals itself to be even more intrusive. Though still based on *nonsense*, among its many theatrical references it hints at a Becket brand of existentialism. This did not mean that Wilson had given up on his obsession with repetition and symmetry: the structural score is still the leading character.

The performance is divided into three parts, corresponding to three different times of the day, from evening to morning, and the orientation of the desolate triangle of earth seen center stage rotates three times from right to left, against a backdrop of a star filled horizon with a very thin lunar crescent. At the top of the triangle there is a structure resembling a sentry box with a glass door. This door opens, and a ray of light escapes, wrapping itself around the stage and setting off a series of visual scales. Their precise temporal rhythms correspond to the musical beats of Tania Leon's classical score or Gavin Bryars' harpsichord, to those of the taped (or merely amplified) vocal arrangement, and to the vague and mysterious solitary whistle we heard before at the beginning of *Edison*.

Everything is connected between one work and another, and among the central characters in this one there is a relationship between a couple that recalls the Berlin production of *D.D.& D.* An older man and woman enter or exit the sentry box, or gravitate over this no-man's land. They are always in symmetrical positions: one seated and the other standing; one facing the audience, the other with his back to the audience. Their prolonged relationship of incommunicability is expressed with absolutely formal perfection, in which every little movement of the hands or fingers is focused on by a spotlight. Just as each scene finds its double, the couple is also duplicated into another, younger couple, who reproduce the same situations and attitudes, sounding a kind of futuristic alarm. We see him flying through the air in the prologue, then later he is hanged in it. Or we see her transfigured into a goddess in the sky and then into an extraterrestrial. The drama seems imminent, within the immobility of memory. But all at once a revolver passes from the hands of the old man to the hands of the woman, who remains alone brandishing the weapon in the center of the stage, which is being torn to pieces by an earthquake. Showers of light rise from deep down in the crevasses and meteorites are slowly lowered. A disturbing apocalyptic at the back of the stage invades this black-and-white production, which has taken from the American fable on which it is based only the vision of the building on top of the mountain. The disturbing sensation is deeply rooted in the supreme image of harmony among light, sound, and movement. It is a sinister expression of an achieved order, of an order that is reality perhaps lost, of unattainable beauty.

FRANCO QUADRI

Jessye Norman in **Great Day in the Morning**, 1982.

Scene plan by Robert Wilson for the two acts.

la maison dans la forêt

la maison dans la forêt

l'ombre

les jonquilles

la forêt au matin

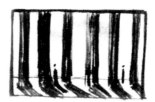

le lac

la chambre

le feu

l'orchidée

l'arbre calciné

la maison dans la forêt

la chambre

la maison dans la forêt

38

In the blues
with Jesse Norman

The opera opened in Munich three years after Wilson's debut. It was during a period in which the preparation of *the CIVIL warS* was already well underway and, between performances, the artist also held various preparatory workshops in different locations and with different troupes. It was also time in which Wilson established contact with certain celebrities for whom he felt the naive enthusiasm of a fan. Among them were opera stars such as Hildegarn Behrens, who participated in the Freiburg workshop, and Jesse Norman, who materialized in October 1982 at the Théatre des Champs Elysées in *Great Day in the Morning*, a show produced for her by Robert Wilson on the theme of black American music. The great black soprano also selected the pieces, uniting a classic collection of spirituals with gospel music, ballads, work songs, blues, plus a touch of jazz, in two acts which together lasted three hours. Wilson tried to reconstruct an imaginary day of slavery, playing on the slowness of the rhythms. The show was uneven, however, because of a decline in the quality of the musical intervals (by Charles Lloyd Jr.) and the choral pieces, with their enormous floral, even forestal backgrounds in which survivors of *Uncle Tom's Cabin* find themselves struggling with invasions of fog and sparks.

Poetic emotion was mustered, however, when the great diva stood alone at the front of the stage, her shadow projected on the gray paneling in the background, or when she stood at an enormous window facing a starry blue sky, or reclined on a petrified tree, while in the background a procession of human black triangles wearing hoods crossed the stage against the light. Here her splendid voice connected perfectly with her minute and implacable gestures, emphasized by the light; an arm that slowly rises and falls, a majestic lifting of her shoulders, the movement with infinitesimal rhythm towards a small table in front of a dark window in the sharp finale. Her vital energy pours with persistent indifference like water from a carafe into an overflowing glass, symbolic but concrete like all her gestures and poses, in a time that is real and which she makes her own once again.

The Olympic Games
and an architect of time

Apart from its internal structural geometry, which anticipates the complex geographical organization of *the CIVIL warS*, *Die Goldenen Fenster* relied once again on the concept of repetition expanding beyond the confines of a single show. The work, which was produced in its entirety only in Munich, previously had been planned as part of a multiple serial of five simultaneous creations to be performed in five different countries, each one having its own version. The real show would therefore have consisted in the globality of the five performances–an elusive prolongation of the work in space (but in temporal harmony, different time zones permitting), with the hypothetical repetition of possible comparisons already seen, for example, in the two parts of both *Patio* and *D.D.& D.*, and in the first and fourth acts of *Edison.*

It was a prelude to the great multinational fresco of *CIVIL warS*, or more precisely *the CIVIL warS: a tree is best measured when it is down*, launched as "the greatest show on earth" and scheduled as a worldwide performance at the Olympics in Los Angeles in 1984. It would be the culmination of a work that took four years to complete (two years of study and two years of actual preparation, including partial productions), six parts created and produced in six different countries and on three continents, an estimated 250 actors, twelve hours duration (reducible to nine), and five million dollars budgeted (to be increased according to need). The segments of the production are considered self-sufficient and autonomous due to combining of genres–lyrics, prose, dance, cinema, painting, oriental theater. Each is an example of total theater which expresses itself in the same way as in an American opera, and encourages the Olympic spirit not only toward brotherhood among heterogeneous and international forces, but also toward a reunification with history and toward overcoming barriers.

The first staged production of the project at Freiburg goes back to 1982. With the joint efforts of both the theater and the university, Wilson succeeded in obtaining a space which he used as a stage for a month with about eighty "volunteers," composed of his veteran actors, students of dramatic art schools, and new actors deliberately taken on for the show. So in the course of two weekends, thanks to his faithful followers, the *Project* came to life, almost in its entirety, perhaps for the one and only time. It first came about on paper, thanks to myriad drawings which were hung on the walls in living rooms turned into showrooms. The drawings reveal the stages of the gigantic operation, specifying the fundamental divisions into shows, acts and sections, while a system of small models was used to visualize the complicated scenography. Meanwhile, in an endless session of explanations and discussions, the *stagiaires* read the texts and traced the fabric of the actions, or better, they acted them out using elementary methods: climbing up a step ladder to indicate a tree while, lacking taped audio back-up, a small chorus sang a melody.

The process was medieval, the results fascinating. The slowed-action style recalled early Wilson, and later the Jessye Norman period, but it was still unique given its new context. The production aimed to create visual effects using the most sophisticated technological methods: computerized stage movements, lights capable of emphasizing with millimetric rays the minutest gesture, ultrasensitive amplifications of multi-track tapes with dolby-type diffusion. With a technique more often used in the fashion world than in the theater, and more commonly on Broadway than for the subject in question–after all, what was being "sold" was still *avant-garde*–the show was destined for a more cosmopolitan audience of "buyers," theater and festival directors, cultural ministers and attaches, female financial backers, heiresses, and sponsors of all kinds.

Beyond the aesthetic achievements of *CIVIL warS*, the story of its genesis cannot be told without also telling of the dreams, the neuroses, the trials, the journeys, the contacts, the entirely alienated days of its creator. And add to that the weight of the shows already produced and those that were still ideas, theatrical performances in production, plans for television versions, plans for a series of publications and exhibitions of drawings and other props that accompany Wilson's shows, and the miles of tapes and recordings of the soundtrack made by a sound engineer who soon became the director's shadow. Nor can we forget the progressive remodelings following the display of names of famous actors and then their immediate eclipse: from David Bowie (once a candidate to play Lincoln) to Hildegarde Behrens (who was present in Freiburg), to the faithful Jessye Norman, to the sudden apparition of the names of Delphine Seyrig and Ilideo Kanze. And finally, the obliterations, among these the big battle act, which was to take place on several levels covering the entire stage and divided in four parts like a cross.

In fact the show was larger than the stage, or the multiple stages, and identified itself finally with the *Project*; for this multimedia opera falls into that category of artistic creations which are exempt from the limitations of time or space. The basic character of this *Project* we have seen before and its elements include the following: the layout of the production, the endless spider web traced among various capital investments in the production, the economic relationship between the theater and its sponsors, the interweaving of the two acts that make up each section—in short, the entire technical and organizational unit itself becomes important in the sense of expression. For this colossal production "*à la* Lucas" (whose galactic *Star Wars* is found in the title), for this ephemeral cathedral destined to be built thanks to contributions from various communities in successive periods of time, Wilson patiently puts together pieces of a mosaic in a varied unified system that reminds us of only one architect of time, namely Cristo, for whom the process is as significant as the result.

Today we can talk about the completion of the work, even though like many of the cathedrals, it never was completed. The French and Japanese sections were never produced. And though they were exported in reviews and tournees, the three European episodes fully produced in Rotterdam, Cologne, and Rome, and the "knee plays" performed in Minneapolis, never reached the Olympic finish line. In the end the Olympic Arts Festival decreased the guaranteed percentage, indispensable for meeting on-site production costs, while various contributing national theaters came through with their respective production costs, showing a sense of political-cultural responsibility that evidently escaped the Olympic Committee. In fact, Los Angeles refused even to show a transmission via satellite of a performance that took place elsewhere and was proposed by the Schauspielhaus in Cologne. But we must not get carried away by newspaper gossip and forget our sense of utopia.

Model and scene from act I of
the CIVIL warS, Cologne 1984.

War and peace with "knee plays": the fragments of utopia

Embracing diverse nationalism and time periods, *the CIVIL warS* was a blend of mythology and eclecticism. On the one hand, there were the Minneapolis "kneeplays," which were conceived as introductions to individual acts in shows, such as the intermissions performed by Childs and Sutton in *Einstein*, then gathered together and produced in a single performance. They refer to manual labor, and in one a tree is chopped down (hence the composition's subtitle: *a tree is best measured when it is down*) after which the wood itself undergoes numerous metamorphoses. On the other hand, there was the larger theme of civil strife, but a more restrictive criteria was used for its representation. The American Civil War and the thirty-year Central European war made the cut, but the Roman prototype, the Russian Revolution, and the French Revolution were ignored; Frederick the Great comes on stage, along with the Samurai and the American Indians, Henry VI and Garibaldi, Benjamin Franklin, and Jules Verne, in addition to endless herds of animals, mixed in with famous personalities from Mata Hari to Madame Curie, as well as literary characters such as Don Quixote, Captain Nemo, or Scarlett O'Hara dressed up as Minnie Mouse and destined to be played by an actress from the Kabuki Theatre in the Tokyo piece, alas never produced.

But this *Reader's Digest* version of the history of humanity, to be appreciated mostly for its powerful visual effect, is gradually put aside by the invasion of nature, first by the appearance of animals, then with the triumph of plantlife. This was particularly evident in an unfortunate section created to close the cycle, produced at the Teatro dell'Opera in Rome, with repetitions by Philip Glass directed by Marcello Panni. The comparisons among similars are left to episodic spurts, and these *CIVIL warS* become an account of the struggle for survival and the conflict between man and nature, concluding with a generic appeal for peace and a naive plunge into ecology.

Storyboard by Robert Wilson for **Knee Plays**, Minneapolis 1984.

This plunge appears anachronistic. The Roman ending takes us back to Arcadia, in a highly atmospheric scene created by the smooth flow of various layers of theater curtains upon which are reproduced tropical botanical flora. The gods of Olympus walk among them while they sing, led by Hercules Furens, patron of the Olympics, who sings Seneca in a tenor voice, accompanied by an oleographic torch bearer. In the background, however, remains the armor-plating of a spaceship with a porthole out of which peer first General Lee, then a young Mrs. Lincoln dressed in black. The drowning of history in culture is a recurrent theme in the episodes produced by the great Kermesse.

The German episode, which marks the beginning of Wilson's collaboration with Heiner Müller, is more ambitious and is even more resistant to synthesis, with its five-hour length and its wide range of topics in the scenes between the first and fourth acts. The opening act is futuristic, with two astronauts rotating on two very high metal ladders (similar to those used in the Rome production, from which Hercules and Abraham Lincoln descend), while the dark continent outlined in the background is destined to stay afloat in pieces after a very violent spark ignites it, clearly alluding to an atomic catastrophe. With representational power that is not easy to forget, there are two striking war scenes: an attack led by Frederick the Great, which ends on a tapestry of death, and a swarming, desolate, Flemish-like image of an encampment immersed in the fog and boredom of daily routine.

The second part develops towards an elementary ideological position: a screen is lowered—an allusion to the Berlin Wall—and onto it are projected sequences of marine and animal life. On both sides of the screen are characters representing the eminent figure of Frederick of Prussia (and his consort), one of Wilson's frequent subjects, busy making historical speeches. Here Wilson revives a style rooted in canonic rituals, taken from the days of the Open Theatre. We find ourselves, perhaps too insistently and too obviously, before a triple confrontation with history, daily life, and nature. However, the verbosity of the dialogue and the weighty imposition of paradigm assume a provocative function: together with passages from his own *Gundling*, Müller scatters citations from the Bible to Shakespeare, from Goethe to Hölderin, and the direction has him speak in a neutral manner, without any attempt at explanations or interpretations. On the other hand, a break from genius is not lacking—actors and bit players in gaudy costumes come one by one to the front of the stage and form a square on the podium before the audience. They are motionless, with disturbing grimaces on their faces like something out a surrealist painting.

In the Rome production, the naturalistic enchantment of the green hills of the Shouwburg in Rotterdam was gone. The hills had been a figurative backdrop to a stage furrowed by a stream first silver with ice, then blue, first filled with ice skaters, then with toy sailboats, surrounded by bundles of wheat or a carpet of red tulips, while a white bear amuses himself and a child enters the world of fairy tales, except when he remembers to tell us all about his day. The action takes place horizontally, always in the same direction, along parallel layers, instilling a sense of time, while together with the changing of the seasons, history is pursued: the tireless march of a wounded veteran, Mata Hari being conducted to her death by hooded executioners, appearances by the folkloric Queen Wilhelmina, the mythical William the Silent, and with a nod to Barnum, "the biggest woman in the world," four meters tall, dressed in black, with the face of Sheryl Sutton. The anxiety involved in creating a show in which there are many overlapping themes, five alternating languages, a soundtrack that tends towards ballet music, and to top it all of, so as not to ignore Ruisdael, the sense of a "Dutch image," is felt everywhere. The principal danger faced by the ensemble of Rotterdam in terms of the overall production was the exhaustive and chilling aesthetics of the piece which, drawn out over nine hours, could have been fatal for the audience.

Besides the many cross references among the various episodes and Wilson's signature tone of detachment and rarification, from all directions one sees the mark of eclecticism. This is also because the project is based on a universal plan which includes the diversity of national expression and theatrical experience. Rotterdam offered cinematic cadences and atmosphere, Cologne cosmic greatness of total theater in its strikingly impressive opening and its set designs for prose pieces, while Rome, for all intents and purposes, recorded the achievement of lyric opera, a dream of Wilson's ever since *Einstein* (not to mention *Queen Victoria*). Thanks to the score by Philip Glass, the rehearsal phase of *Medea* by Gavin Bryars was finally recorded and was being produced parallel to *CIVIL warS*. In Cologne it was also Glass who provided a taped score, while in Rotterdam the sound for music and voices was coordinated by the Cipriot Nicolas Economou, while the work of Bryars and the Japanese Jo Kondo went unused, and the Marseilles and Tokyo productions never happened.

David Byrne composed the hypnotic and evocative music, including a score for brass instruments based on pieces for a New Orleans jazz band, for *Knee Plays*, the collage of in-between-act skits elaborated with a Japanese flavor in Minnesota. The orchestra and singers of the songs, also written by Byrne, were located in a covered partition off to one side of the stage, according to the rules of *bunraku*, an obscure historical form of puppet theater which these knee players promoted to the status of a performance. A group of dancers wearing hoods like the stage hands on oriental theater work the poetic automatons, often hanging by strings and created by Wilson, according to the slow sophisticated dynamism of the magical choreography of Suzushi Hanayagi. They lead them into an attack on the skeletal sets made of paper and bamboo depicting the story of a tree in the form of the letter T, where a man, in fear of a lion, has climbed in order to read a book. As the tree slowly falls, the trunk turns into a wooden cabin and then into a boat, it meets a bird, undergoes a canon attack, and sinks, only to resurface in the jungle, adorned with writings that will inspire a book from which a tree will grow.

White on white, with refined geometric figures and inimitable rhythms, this homage to a great theatrical civilization to which Wilson has always, for many reasons, felt indebted, reveals itself as an isolated and naive

Howie Seago in **The Forest**, 1988.

Alcestis, 1986. Drawing by Robert Wilson for scene 3A, act I.

gemstone compiled from what were thought to be only skits, and brings a powerful message addressed to the mess of war, but above all to the complications created by technology.

Under the sign
of Heiner Müller

The hyperactivity of the Olympic adventure has Wilson hooked and, in any case, by now it would be impossible to pull out of a work already being produced on several fronts. Further developing his taste for multiples, he makes a choice that will cause him to confront his ideas organically for the first time in terms of the classics. He mounts two operatic productions of *Medea* with the music of Charpentier and Bryars, respectively, and takes on Euripedes in *Alcesti*, produced for the American Repertory Theatre. The latter is a conventional exercise sustained by the charm of bright geometrical figures, and serves as an introduction to the lyrical version by Gluck for the Staatsoper in Stuttgart. The text of the tragedy is drastically reduced and parts of it are transferred to a bourgeois setting, while other parts are transformed into a grotesque farce. The director centers the production around the regret for the lack of music and on the contract (a topic dear to him) between what we see and what we hear. The fulcrum is still the visual element. Behind a magically transparent wall/curtain is a landscape of crumbling rocks (which will be transformed in the end of a laser). A river runs through the landscape, and in the distance there are three cypress trees that will change into columns or smokestacks, emblems of a hypothetical future city. After a surreal banquet, Alcesti returns, concealed beneath a veil, and is replicated into three versions of herself, one for each day that Admeto must pass before he is able to unveil her mysterious nature. The other characters duplicate themselves as well and their actions are repeated in an intriguing process, while the multivoiced gestures of the chorus are very effective, and draw upon the pictorial world of Paul Delvaux, in a setting that takes us back to Rousseau's *Il Doganiere*.

The dialogue is spoken or shouted in different tones of voice, and the landscape corresponds to the harmonic resonance of a monologue added as an introduction by Heiner Müller, but which actually resounds throughout the entire production. It is the presentation of a work entitled *Description of a Picture*, which refers to the stage set. A text is first recited off stage by Wilson himself or by one of his collaborators, with echoes, layerings, repetitions, and then simply pronounced without emotion by a character who is bandaged like a mummy, suspended in mid-air at the left of the stage, and practically in the lap of an enormous ancient statue shining in the dark. The contamination of ancient or primitive repertories of different origins is the thematic basis here, and seems to want to negate the possibility of salvaging tradition, but by adapting the text in a sensitive way Müller brings it to life again in a new cool and intellectually composed image.

Müller is not present only as playwright, repeating his Cologne experience with *CIVIL warS*: at times the diversity of formation and culture serve to reinforce intelligence. The writer from the DDR prefers formal prediction to the rigorously interpretive approach of the American artist. Wilson, in turn, is enchanted by the informal writing of this manipulator of antiquity. After the baptism of *Alcesti*, the first texts that Wilson puts on stage are by Müller. And at the Theatre der Welt 1987 in Stuttgart, *Quartett* revives the mocking unseemliness of *Les Liaisons dangereuses*, extracted from the rubble of time, using contrasting forms resulting in one of Wilson's more extreme stagings. The ironic verbal duel between Lados's two main characters, who play with sexual perversions until they form a duet of inverted roles, takes place in an abstract frame with a net that separates the lead actors; and three other characters, who do not speak, are of various ages, acting out some of the actions the main characters allude to, emphasizing the willful banality of it all through the use of bright Warholian colors, aesthetic formality, and exhaustive repetition of same leitmotif.

Hamletmaschine, produced in German at the Thalia Theatre and in English at New York University, brings us back to Hamlet and Ophelia as relics transported along with their frenzied monologues *à la* Ezra Pound to the time of Coca Cola (but also to the time of the Berlin wall). "Hamlet is Germany," the author said, citing Ferdinand Freiligrath, a German writer and friend of Marx, but then added his own motivation for this judgment. "He never knows what to decide, nor why he always makes the wrong decision." For Wilson, *Hamletmaschine* represents a dreamlike world with acquatic clarity, the memory of an immutable and lost classicism. Beginning with textual allusions, he constructs elementary action with characters who take turns entering on stage, each one assigned specific movements, and then become frozen in the act of lifting an arm or opening the mouth to shout. Performed

47

the first time in silence, the action is repeated, and musical beats are added one by one up to five, which is the number of sections comprising this brief, dark piece. Each time, however, the perspective and the few objects on stage are moved forty-five degrees. One wall is covered by a white screen while the others remain black, but events do not change, even though they are recomposed each time with new gestures and new details, and revealed by the attribution of words which come from a relentless machine, the one of the title, that suddenly springs to life. This was a little harsh for the rationalist French (I saw the performance at the Festival d'Automne) and they almost accused Wilson of having lobotomized Müller. The author, whose portrait, like a caption beneath a painting, is ripped up during the performance, likes the solution because it allows him "to enter into a world that is very personal." It is a world that, due to the constant repetition, makes one think of *Morel's Invention* by Bioy Casares, in which a machine stops time and makes the characters repeatedly relive moments captured from their lives, not unlike the survivors from Elsinore, who are like phantoms among the ruins of Europe, never able to die.

The same repetitive technique occurs in certain parts of *Death Destruction & Detroit II*, a show that continues the series begun eight years before with *D.D.& D.*, also at the Schaubühne. Added to Müller's contributions are those of the director's two regular collaborators, Maita di Niscemi and Cynthia Lubar. Following the imaginary life of Rudolph Hess, which was produced in the old theater, comes a detailed biography of Kafka constructed through citations—not always entirely comprehensible—from his work. The continuity with the preceding work—some parts of which show up in the new—is seen in the formal contrast, like positive and negative, between different scenes in the first part and the same scenes in the second part, or between the black which dominates the stage and the white of the sketched partitions that cover the walls. All four of the partitions can be moved around the revolving seats of the audience. The two lateral partitions are the ones that are used most often in symmetrical movement during the performance, while the gradated front partition rises like a stairway, and is the place from which long monologues are delivered.

Apart from these rare moments of stillness, the figurative representation that takes place moves in a slow dream-like, almost delirious, rhythm. While a faint recording is heard in the background, like an echo or a burst of everyday noises, different reincarnations of K. appear. We experience the claustrophobia of a railroad train compartment. We watch as a replica of K's study alternates with the anguish of traffic, reduced in the audience to a pair of automobile headlights shining directly on them. Or we see the persistent advance of an unstable spaceship, or an enormous white mouse, or a man flying through the air, or a bear walking up the wall, or a threatening black panther with eyes like burning embers. Under a sky pierced by Caravaggesque beams of light, we see a gallery of wax statues, intended to represent slices of life. To this maze-like mosaic world, which will be described in long discourse in the second act, familiar characters return while endless dancing continues. An old witness displays his silent agony for almost the entire four-and-a-half hours of the show. Thunder and lightning come and go in cycles, as do alarming messages of great poetic invention.

Certainly more poetic than what will happen in the final chapter of Wilson's collaboration with Müller, *The Forest* is a prehistoric colossus created for the Berlin Capital of Culture 1988, planned to go together with a film by Wim Wenders that was never produced. The text, created in collaboration with Carryl Pinckney, is less brilliant, however, than others (for example, Byrne's music), and not much is memorable from this epic by Gilgamesh, except for the performances by the still-very-young Martin Wuttke, some scenes choreographed by Suzushi Hanayagi in the style of *Deafman Glance*, and the parade of antediluvian animals reintroduced by Shiraz. But the reading of the poem sounds more ecological than philosophical, and no matter how open one is to being transported between eras, the contrast between a savage Enkidu howling like Tarzan and a bourgeois Gilgamesh who takes advantage of love to tyrannically impose the corruption of progress, is hard to digest. In a more comical spirit, the two heroes straddle their chairs like horses, while at a small nearby table, dressed like a goddess, the terrible American mother reads destiny's plan in her cards as shouts of "Death to mothers!" are heard.

Two, three, a hundred "Orlandos"

We are living at a time when one can find even in a show like *The Forest* a nostalgic side to it, and in this case the nostalgia is for Robert Wilson, the creator. With regard to his pieces and their lyrics, especially during the flowering of his German career, he is the creative interpreter, even though more than a thousand times when talking about a performance he has affirmed that interpretation is up to the audience, while it is up to the director and the critics to "ask the questions." And it is not at all certain that in his work the predominance of the image is destined to disappear, or even that it will lose its determined autonomy. In the field of drama, the director has succeeded in making a unique place for himself, and without excluding at least some reference to actual theatrical texts. He put on an Ibsen (*When We the Dead Detest Ourselves*) and a Buchner (*Death of Danton*) in America, a one-act play by Chekov in Munich, a *Swan Song*, conceived as dialogue *à la* Bernhard but ending up in the arms of Beckett. Nonetheless, he invented and plowed his own field of literature, finding the material for his shows preferably in novels or short stories, to be produced as monologues or dialogues, especially for two characters.

Orlando by Virginia Woolf is transformed into a two-hour work from more than two hundred pages, covering a time period of almost four centuries, which was lived, paradoxically, in thirty-six years by the extraordinary bisexual character of the title. Since the work involves only one actress and a literary theme, it is inevitable that Edith Clever's name would come to mind, specialized as she was in non-theatrical 'talking' works of art under the direction of Syberberg, like *Le Marquise von ...* by Kleist. Jutta Lampe, the actress chosen for *Orlando*, and Clever are the two great women of the German stage and the Schaubühne.

In contrast to Kleist's approach to a text, the adaptation by Wilson together with Pinckney is not faithful to the text, but is a rigorous reorganization in which the less narrative parts (and also some fundamental characters) are sacrificed from this complex novel/essay. It is somewhat painful to see the literary power of the work confined to the background while the actress impulsively searches for the meaning of life in time. In a monologue, Orlando confirms the existential direction of the production. The character uses an informal first-person language, while in the original the voice is in the third person and conveys a detachment and irony with regard to the unrestrained *divertissement* of the action, thereby emphasizing the presence of the authoress. The book is dedicated to Vita Sackville-West, who was the model for Orlando. Dressed in the clothes of one of her aristocratic ancestors, she becomes the androgynous protagonist who lives as a young boy in the Elizabethan era and wakes up as a woman during the Restoration in Turkey. Calmly astride the two sexes, she soars above the snobbism and disguises of all literary societies, but actually relates the story of only one.

Lampe appears as a malicious page of the Queen, then gradually becomes more feminine. While she goes behind the tree of life suspended half a meter above the stage, the final sex change takes place while a deafening sound suggests an invisible mirror shattering into many pieces. Thereafter the actress begins to look more like Virginia than Vita, albeit abstractly, and the back-drop is in a continuous state of flux in which white plays with black in an attempt to preserve at least one of the many dualities with which the novel constantly plays. Curtains adorned with *chiaroscuro* figures run along the background or foreground enveloping the ascetic space that devoured the furnishings and decorations so important to the narration, while pieces of linear furniture come and go, in an infinite mental time, to the sound of distant music.

After having recited some verse by Sappho in Greek, and after finding in her hand a glass globe that is also a skull, like a Faust who is also Hamlet, Jutta Lampe begins the series of clothing changes (designed by Susanne Raschig) and above all changes of expression. She embarks on a neurotic journey of physical exercise, using a technique already elaborated by the director together with Müller, the rhythmic anguish of which soon causes her to lose her voice. She encounters some magic moments, like when she finds at her feet a miniature door that opens and closes, taking her suddenly to the time of the monstrous Alice, and she is immediately swallowed up by the pages of the book. Ultimately, Lampe prevails because the show essentially consists of her exceptional performance as an actress capable of achieving any transfiguration through words.

Almost four years later in Lausanne at the Theatre Vidy, and then in Paris, Milan, etc., Wilson gives the same part to Isabelle Huppert and uses an identical stage set. The soundtrack is also the same, alternating distant musical auras with allusive noises, in an empty visual space created with all-enveloping, painted curtains made of monochrome panels whose movements can be regulated. In this conceptual whirlpool, tiny toy objects or a back-lit black staircase with drawers for steps may materialize. From above, the trunk of the oak tree of life is lowered, along with a white sheet, both curved and rigid, like the wings of an angel. The gray, moody tonality of the stage is devoured by the struggle between the colors of day and night, which follow and alternate with each other, remodeling the scene without stopping the action and redesigning the atmosphere through a game of radiating lights and shadows.

In Wilson's perfectionist theater, the sound element and the visual element are taken up again and repeated, and are to be considered in correlation with the textual element and the human element, and all their variants. The verbal text is translated into a smooth and fluid French version by the Shakespearean specialist Jean-Michel Deprats, who maintains the adaptation as reductive form, as well as the existential posture of the protagonist, clearly not represented in a naturalistic manner. The human instrument does not "interpret" the heroine, nor does she embody her even if she speaks for her and exemplifies her, at times even showing signs of identifying with her. The text, then, should result in a correspondence of words to a code of deliberate gestures to be reflected upon in a formal way. The descriptiveness of the script is realized, however, in the infinitive present, the *hic et nunc* of the stage, through deliberate intricacy and with incessant breaking up of gestures: a journey of the body into the light.

Even though the script is scrupulously identical, why is the show produced in Lausanne so different? Because this *Orlando* is a story created for an actress who talks about Orlando, and because Wilson works on the body, the nerves, and on the evocative and autonomous introspection of this actress. Due to the language, in place

Two scenes from **La Maladie de la Mort** with Michel Piccoli, Lausanne 1996.

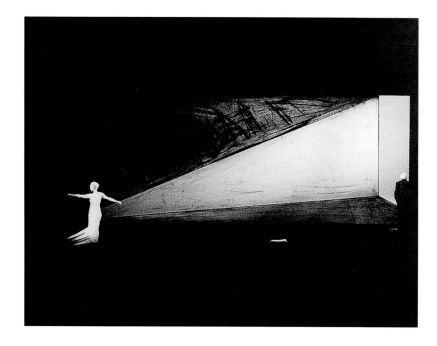

of the solemn Lampe, who makes a sensational impression but who lacks playfulness, they substitute the emotional and sensitive approach of Huppert, who is available for any role, including ironic parodies. In Huppert's rendition every perspective is revealed and every perception is fresh from the opening scene, when lying on Procuste's little bed, the actress bubbles over, singing like a bird, until the finale when, lying down again, she covers herself with bird feathers, saying at first an apocryphal "J'étais seul" and then a conclusive, arbitrary "Je suis seule." Throughout the piece what should change is the condition of the actress, and this actress does not seem to have the stature when she presents herself as a little boy dressed like a page, she doesn't seem to have a face except to show bewildered emotion during carnival time in the London of James I, she does not seem to have any sex when, upon waking and finding herself transformed in the Orient, she contemplates her feet and listens to her own voice as she tries to hit a high note. She narrates history as she walks back and forth across the stage followed by the light, never stopping her march, her arm continuously outstretched, perhaps in the thrall of those eternal silent moments. She drifts through the centuries, feeling completely at ease as she takes off her dress, under which she is wearing a new splendid costume from a different era. Looking for a non-existent heart, like the one looked for in vain in the onion of Peer Gynt, she swims, skates, goes horseback riding, crawls on her knees, lays down, before signing her name with a finger in the air. And like a chameleon she makes herself disappear, while also realizing herself in the exasperating and endless continuity of change, cultivated in substantial immobility.

And yet this actress, so iridescent in her expressions and physical appearance during the 135 minutes of the evening, succeeds in making herself over five months later in Milan at the Festival del Teatro d'Europa, after finishing two cycles of performances in Paris at the Odeon. In an excellent interpretation of this mental mosaic, she constructed an improved and more complete image of the piece's immediate reality, while bringing a vibrant energy to its informal size. She succeeded in executing with absolute precision the maze of movements and intonations, while pouring out the sensitivity that animates and even contradicts her, reaffirming herself bit by bit, allowing herself an excursion in acting virtuosity, taking hold of this absolutely abstract project with majestically creative freedom.

I saw reflected in her character the same condition of the actress, who lives only for the theater, nourishing herself with the surprise that originates from the mystery of the stage, thereby making a musical-literary *pastiche* into a stage production. The result is astonishing, and one to which the subconscious cannot be indifferent. Huppert obtained, through her femininity, the force of the masculine side of the character, while the opposite phenomenon occurred with the apparently more masculine Lampe–who always leaves her indelible imprint on her characters–that of a more intense image of the woman. It is this transformation that has always intrigued Wilson–where two figures complete each other in time and space. And the possibilities are not limited to these two actresses: Susse Wold played the role in a 1993 Danish version in Copenhagen, directed by Katrine Wiedemann; the English version starred Miranda Richardson in the 1996 Edinburgh Festival. Repeating the success of *Orlando* in international multiples, Wilson had plans to include the colorless but by no means less diabolical duet from *La Maladie de la Mort* by Marguerite Duras, with music by Hans Peter Kuhn, from Berlin 1991 to Lausanne 1996.

Parody of musicals or German rock opera?
Three aces for *The Black Rider*

Moving away from the re-use of literature, besides dipping into his own personal repertory and his continued active presence at opera houses, Wilson returns to his preferred genre and invents musicals *sui generis*, associating himself, as is his specialty, with grand and unpredictable partners. With the Thalia Theater in Hamburg as headquarters and a debut date set for March 1990, he mobilized his three aces, himself included, who amounted to three decades of non-conformist American art: William S. Burroughs as script writer of 'retro' conscience; Tom Waits, whose music reflects his star-quality charisma; and Wilson himself, as bridge and mediator in the creation of yet another formally German show, notwithstanding its American spirit, with actors who could sin in English and a vocation for the international tour. But besides those involved, this was not the usual million dollar colossus, as proven by its short rehearsal period. Noble influences are not lacking from *The Black Rider* (subtitled *The Casting of the Magic Bullets*). Elements of *The Sniper Hunter* by Weber and Thomas de Quancey, are translated into a rock opera performed by an eight-piece chamber music orchestra. The declared objective is a musical which aims to parody certain parodies of Broadway, such as *The Phantom of the Opera*, or West-End cult shows in the style of *The Rocky Horror Picture Show.*

At the Thalia Theater, a temple to prose theater located in the rainy Hanseatic city dear to Gustav Grundgens's *Faust*, and thus to Mephisto, the devil takes center stage. The show opens with all the characters leaping out of a black coffin, which lies fallen on a smoky fog-filled stage like the monolith in *2001: A Space Odyssey*, only to turn up again in the second act in a cemetery of skulls and bones as if in a remake of *Nosferatu.* The limping devil, impeccable in his white, black, and red suits, is played in different vampiresque versions by the excellent actor Dominique Horwitz, who, when not in the scene, directs the action from the prompter's position, perhaps with flaming fingers or with a bright red ear. In the scene, marked at the beginning by the closing of an enormous black screen, the devil's sidekick or double–a bisexual witch or devil with a thick lock of hair covering half of his face–appears, as does a possessed ancestor who peers out from an expressionist picture frame from which point, changing position and perspective, he follows the action with a smirk on his face like Boris Karloff. As the words of the first song, "We'll have a gay old time," are somewhat ambiguously announced, we plummet into the gaiety of the past. A scribe wants to marry the daughter of the lord of the manor. The lord of the manor, however, wants for his son-in-law a hunter who, like the ancestor in the portrait, is much talked about for a presumed pact with the devil.

The young scribe studies hard to pass a qualifying exam but doesn't get any of the answers right. After he dances a polka with his girlfriend and lifts her high into the sky, a gun appears in mid-air like a shimmering mirage. He grabs it, and without hesitation, succumbs to the devil's flattery. As a consequence, all he has to do is lift the gun barrel and vultures, geese, doves all fall to earth, or like at a carnival, cut-outs of a herd of deer topple as they're hit, or threatening shadows seen behind the curtain are shot down. As soon as there are no more bullets left, the "sniper hunter" suffers the torment of abstinence since, as one of the songs says, "the magic bullets leads to the devil, like marijuana leads to heroin."

Burroughs comes out on the side of prohibition, without omitting a personal reference, since Wilhelm (that is, William, like Burroughs and Shakespeare) is the name of the scribe, to whom the happy ending of Weber's opera is denied. The final bullet, fired during the prematrimonial antidoping exam, instead of hitting the white dove sitting in the black tree, turns back satanically like a boomerang and hits his fiancee, not unlike what happened to the author of *Naked Lunch* forty years before in Mexico when, like William Tell, he aimed a gun at a glass on top of his wife's head, killing her when the shot missed.

Bob Wilson amuses himself in turn by manipulating the heavily made-up characters as if they were in a silent vampire film (an evil character from *Star Wars* also makes an appearance). He makes them move like marionettes from the pages of an antique book of fables, among chairs and tables of changing proportions. Pine trees in the background shrivel and curl into themselves, while Chinese shadows scurry, pastel-colored lasers beam, and the wind whistles. During the between-act skit, we catch a glimpse of the full moon, watch the witches' sabbath explode, see coffins fly through the air, and the enchanted stones shine once more. Beneath a giant bat we see a parade of women with heads like owls, like Egyptian goddesses. There is a Halloween-party atmosphere which, in its happier moments takes us back to the exhilarating spirit (though a bit dated) of the Ridiculous Theatre, or of old musical reviews from off-off Broadway.

A company of German actors, who perform in their own language and sing, their voices amplified, in English, work with enthusiasm and seek out comic effects. They satisfy to the best of their ability the melodic rhythms of the twelve songs by Waits, at least two of which are extremely communicative. The orchestral music resembling a movie soundtrack becomes embarrassing in the second act, when the music takes over entirely and the characters turn into mute little children, having already exhausted a rather stale repertory. In the end, everyone climbs back into the coffin from which they first came, accompanied by a series of painted canvasses on a string, like sheets hanging out to dry; they are sketches for scenes, prepared by Wilson, which high production costs prevented him from realizing. So, with the spirit of a university student, and within the compromises of a dilettante perfectionist, the director from Texas created, somewhat surprisingly, a consumer's product.

The Black Rider was destined to be continued. Again, in collaboration with Tom Waits, *Alice* arrived two years later, as usual at the Thalia, for Christmas in Hamburg. The scenography of *Alice*, a little weak, by Paul Schmidt, rests on the sexually mysterious relationship between Charles Dogdson (Lewis Carroll) and his pupil. The music is tired but there are some splendid scenes, thanks to the director, who looks at himself through Carroll, and who gives us dazzling visions of a dream-like Wonderland often on the edge of nightmare. Wilson enjoys himself by mounting notice boards with word puzzles to remind us that the entire show is a puzzle, as is demonstrated by the structural care he takes in perfectly matching the first and second acts, centering around the speech and the triumph of images. The chapter, *Time Rocker*, appearing in June 1996, calls on Lou Reed to give an imaginary history of rock. The criteria for assemblage and distribution is similar to that of *Black Rider* and *Alice*. The director succeeds once again in pulling off one of his great cyclical caprices: the blending of three Hamburg operas, three love stories of changing inspiration and musical intensity, in one unique show; first the first three acts, then the second, schematically interwoven, making for the duration and cost of a colossus, which still today no theater can seriously consider.

Playing with the lights
of Gertrude Stein

Wilson's *Faust* could be called "Red Rider" in contrast to "The Black Rider" of Hamburg because of a red Mephistopheles who wraps himself in the curtain. But Wilson had already evoked the intriguing presence of Evil in the mysterious *Maladie de la Mort* by Duras, not to mention the even more Faustian play by Giacomo Manzoni based on the novel by Thomas Mann, produced at La Scala with some fine scenic blending. In *Doctor Faustus lights the lights*, Wilson pays homage to the great mother of American avant-garde theater, as did Richard Foreman when he produced the same piece years ago in Paris. Much loved and constantly plagiarized, Gertrude Stein was his theoretical muse at the start of his career and inspired the blank verse in many of his shows, based on associations and nonsense, and *trompe d'orielle*, or the remolding of endless distortions.

The production was born in April 1992 at the Hebbel Theatre in Berlin, with a company made up of very young pupils, the director's obedient and clearly preferred instruments. In this case they came out of a school in the former DDR and were entirely unaware of the text or its language. They were chosen because of their freedom and freshness as actors beginning at the beginning, reciting in an English that takes on new musical tones as a result of their pronunciation. Nor would a translation have been possible, since as the title reveals, the script is made up of an infinite number of monosyllable and bisyllable word games, where by changing even one consonant the same sounds jump from one verse to the other, like the refrains of an enchanted tongue-twister. What's more, we are dealing with an opera libretto that Gertrude Stein composed in 1938 for a musician in crisis, and revised by Hans Peter Kuhn, so that serial variations alternate amusing arias from musicals and piano sonatas.

The Magician of Lights presents one of his fundamental themes. To acquire, thanks to electricity, the prerogative of changing night into day, this very singular Faust would have sold his soul to the devil, even though we see him in the first scene sending his counterpart literally to hell. It is almost an autobiographical subject for any director, but it is particularly congenial to the creator of *Edison*, whose *Einstein on the Beach* had its apex in a whirl of bright diagrams, and who made famous the image of Rudolf Hess's cell dominated by a giant light bulb in the Berlin production of *D.D.& D.*

Words are the rhythmic protagonist here, and they rebound among the fleshless witticisms of the characters who sagely question their meaning. In the context of parody, Faust accompanies a dog entirely innocent of evil who never stops saying "thank you"–a small child minus the conversations of adults. Margherita–who is also Elena, in fact her name is "Marguerite Ida and Helen Annabel"–is bitten by a snake and cured by a treatment of words by the "Doctor," who is a wizard with rhymes and who, after a legal argument with Mephistopheles, resolves his own problems of going to hell "by himself" simply by going back into the darkness. The verbal score turns into a soundtrack of explosions of amplified voices due to the characters becoming doubles or multiples which, through dynamic counterpoint, completes them. In this way we obtain three Fausts (substituting a nude torso for a jacket to make him appear 'younger'); three Marguerite Idas, etc., two Mephistopheles in red and black, respectively, and then, among others, a Mr. Viper who manipulates a wooden puppet, and a gigantic peasant with a scythe, lifted from a lost Dutch version of *the CIVIL warS*. Wilson responds to the labyrinth of the page by arranging the actors' bodies according to his iron-clad alphabet of gestures. He is consumed by playing with the line between light and shadow, as was Müller in his inventive rehearsals, or as in the graphic sketches of the narrative mentioned above.

The interdependent figures in black and white are arranged by Suzushi Hanayagi's unique choreography within a closed and abstract space. The background of windows or geometric spirals is consonant with a suspended platform, and with lightbulbs of various sizes and intensity hanging from the ceiling and contrasted by a vibrant candle flame. With a purity that recalls Balanchine or Ad Reinhard, the hints at parody dissolve, while the picture continuously renews itself, thanks to the layering of rhythms, and to the use of slow motion and rewind. We are beyond formalism here, and not only because of the vitality and creative pleasure revealed by the show. Certain signs become wounds, like the screaming ascension of a red laser beam that serves to express the bite of a snake, or a strangling gesture around the neck of a spirited dog, or the sealed fate of an impeccable child seen as damaging to harmony. And before darkness leaves Faust alone on the stage, we see him rise, standing out against an ever-narrowing sky on the moveable platform that remains precariously suspended for a long time above the scene. Its shape becomes a disquieting picture of light, while meteorites float like a vision from Kubrik, the final mysterious refraction of a dazzling evening.

A pause for opera

Robert Wilson becomes a sought-after specialist as an opera director, although the canonical traditions of repertory opera present him with some problems. *Salomé* by Strauss for La Scala, which was not much appreciated by the audience, and his oratory formed the action: singers stood motionless on a platform in the foreground while behind them the events unfolded in the form of a pantomime. There was no justification for the mannerist choreography, which ranged from tedious to courageous and was relegated to the background, just as there was no reason to have four dancing Salomés or a few daring sexual fetishes. Especially since the audience only had eyes for the monumental Montserrat Caballé, who was capable of causing chills by accompanying a musical note with a simple partial rotation of his head. Later, in Paris, Wilson's *Martyre de Saint Sebastien*, created an even greater scandal due to the addition of an arbitrary prologue about D'Annunzio and a yacht.

Aside from being an expressive principle, the abstract becomes a defense adopted especially during the more difficult rehearsals. The discourse is brought to the level of expressive rhythm, which does not necessarily 57 coincide with musical rhythm. He carefully establishes a continuous flow for Wagner and a relationship of continuity between "the exterior line and the deep interior line" for Mozart, each work taking place within an essential and geometric space, with a psychological flavor. His operas are a little cold but are livened by the lighting, and gestures never illustrate actions. Each work is identified with a visual scheme that is typical of Wilson and has a rhythm that stresses the modulation of syllables. In *The Magic Flute*, he alternates between the classical and science fiction, and in *Lohengrin*, he inserts a series of monoliths to accompany the different strands of action. In *Butterfly* the stage is empty except for a few Zen objects, and the suicide of Cio-Cio-San represents a moment of great visual emotion enhanced by Suzushi Hanayagi's slow and allusive choreography.

Once upon a time
in Sicily

Once upon a time there were seven hills near Shiraz, where more than twenty years ago, when the Shah of Persia was in power, Bob Wilson performed a miracle for seven days and seven nights. Do you remember *Ka Mountain*? Arriving in Gibellina, a Sicilian town in the region of Belice, entirely rebuilt after an earthquake, I dared to hope that the Texan artist would be able to recreate his Iranian splendor by evoking on the exploded crust of earth one of the symbolic keys to the literature and thought of our century: T.S. Eliot's *The Wasteland* written in 1922, in which he represses anxiety over the power of nature to renew itself among the ruins of antique civilizations. I found, however, that the project had been reorganized: Wilson had abandoned the setting of a debris-covered mountain top for Baglio della Case Di Stefano, a splendidly restored former granary near the artists' quarter above Nuova Gibellina. Thus, he came down from the dead to be among men, finding under those powerful supporting beams the same simple and creative atmosphere of his new atelier on Long Island. And once again he is together with members from his family of artists: Christopher Knowles, the ex-youth grown up thanks to many performances; Maita di Niscemi, the loyal scenographer of Sicilian origin with whom Brad Gooch collaborates this time; the costumist Christophe de Menil; and naturally Philip Glass. These are the many companions with whom to reclimb the stairs of a career, going back to experiment without any urgency for a perfect result, putting himself to the test, in a comfortable environment, where a light goes back to being just a light–who cares if now and again it blinks on and off or simply goes out.

The title of the show, *T.S.E.*, stands for Thomas Stearns Eliot, and the subtitle, *Come under the shadow of this red rock* is a line from *The Wasteland*. It is a work in progress heading eventually to a theater. More than a venture in directing, Wilson creates *his* show, abandoning himself once again to his age-old passion for biography. But the long durations of the old days are over–this time the show is contained in two hours–and he impos-es a rigorous structure on the production. The space is covered with sand from which mirages will appear, as when the show opens and we see twelve old men on twelve gray rocks whispering words taken from the epi-graph to the poem *Satyricon*. Or as in the central movement, when we see, scattered around the figure of the dark, bespectacled Eliot, an ironic series of personalities as monuments repressing history, religion, power, and knowl-edge. The same scene is simultaneously repeated in two areas among the arches, while groups of itinerant spec-tators watch from the shadows.

Despite many allusions, *T.S.E.* does not put the poem, which is unperformable, on the stage. As in preced-ing shows, Wilson relies on biographical details–for example, the period Eliot spent in a rest home in Lausanne, where he wrote *The Wasteland*. Wilson reconstructs hypothetical conversations or apocryphal passages from his other works, and emphasizes citations from the text, visualizing them as the source of inspiration. The creative operation is in the details, the structure, the sensations that Glass's music sustains when he uses and rearranges themes from the past.

The narrative is organized in a symmetrical scheme, within the well-lit spatial geometry. The voice of a read-er or a musician's hammering batons are heard above the multilingual chatter of the forty actors. Before and after the parade of famous historical figures, we follow the poet's imaginative expression of the above-mentioned contact with myth and his beloved medieval period. And we see "neoclassic pop" paintings, expressing once again Wilson's interest in Greece, already seen in *the CIVIL warS*: a black Zeus-like Ade, with his left hand closed inside a box, is in a painting of Persephone being chased towards the abyss, leaving behind the boredom of daily routine; or a young man from the thirteenth century looks out from a painting in a black frame depicting a small lake in the sand, ago-nizing for a rose of white silk, which police-like damsels dressed in white have imprisoned in a wooden container.

Two sequences appear at the opening and reappear with some variation at the end. We see a symbolic and autobiographical family spanning several generations seated at a table, a child called Eliot (or Bob?), and a dog wearing a transparent mask, who sits up and says "Boo," while expedient phrases are interwoven with reminis-cences of Shelley's *Prometheus*. Then come the two "cocktail parties," where the author (who thirty years later writes a play with that title) together with London's intellectual society of 1917, drinks a toast amidst exploding German bombs. With each explosion, all present fall down dead, only to get up again and go on with the cock-tail party, quoting Catullus and listening to Chris Knowles, as an angel with black wings, prophetically repeat "I feel the earth move," as in *Einstein on the Beach*. Out of another cold initial construction, the show embarks on an emotional journey thanks to this surreal fresco, and Wilson's world, a continuous salvaging of the past, actu-ally coincides with that of the other great American in Europe. The truth is artfully revealed to us while banal reality, ritualized by repetition, is overwhelmed by myth.

How to translate Dostoevsky
into abstract theater

Robert Wilson has pursued the phantom of abstract theater for his entire life, always ready to hurl his lance against any naturalistic reproduction of reality. The rigor of his position, which is a constant in his work, has had glorious results in his more important experiments, and in his latest passionate laboratory exercise. His influence, however, on the recitation of monologues or his *pas de deux* should not be neglected, and for the artist it has been a measure of his success with literature; for example, in his approach to Dostoevsky presented at the 1995 Festival d'Automne, the master proposed an admirable example of what he means by an informal reading of a narrative text, translating *The Meek Girl* into a polyphonic and interdisciplinary score. The story had already attracted Bresson for the cinema, and many directors such as Aldo Trionfo for the stage. As always with Dostoevsky, it is the irritating range of psychological variations that strikes theatrical fantasy. The story is about a usurer who tries to understand why his child-wife commits suicide by throwing herself out a window, deeply analyzing their union made up of proud silences, unexpressed blackmail, hidden attraction, and ostentatious contempt. Their relationship was a sado-masochistic hell full of guilt-complexes lived, however, as if on an island of happiness bombarded in fits and starts by a posthumous delirium.

Wilson isolates this situation on a monumental house/stage, all straight lines and sharp corners. A section at the right, tilted towards the flight of steps leading to the audience, has an internal space of smooth shiny wood with four central columns and large windows on three sides looking out at a forest. The architecture, crisp and spare *à la* Hopper, is typical of Wilson in the days of *Edison*. The narrator is multiplied by three: three men looking like Giorgio Armani—hair lacquered straight back, white shirts and severe suits, black shoes, with surrealist accessories and fetishistic images proliferated by the story of the suicide. Their ages are different, as are their gestures and voices. The three actors are an impeccable Robert Wilson, returning to the stage after many years; the young German Thomas Lehmann, who was the splendid lead of *Doctor Faustus*; and Charles Chemin, a small French boy and the son of an actor in *Edison* and *D.D.& D.* and thus second-generation Wilson.

Their lines, enunciated with detachment, are even further distanced by being spoken in their three respective languages. The actors become autonomous parts of the fabric of citations and passages from the text, all frequently repeated, and only at the beginning and at the end do they each propose a translation of the other languages. Attitudes are also mirrored reciprocally, or interact in a system of unrelated dramatic action which is at times pushed towards rhythmic gymnastics, limited to the movements of a well-lit hand or a face slowly turning. Thus, a kind of mute dialogue takes place through a series of sensations that are more evocative than descriptive, often corresponding to suggestions from the soundtrack, with its noises and silences, its rain and thunder, its fire blazes, the beat of an anxious drummer, and the vehement sound of a violin.

Where, in this sensitive, colorful intrigue is the mechanical coldness for which the late Wilson is so often criticized? The code of repeated and varied gestures of pain is woven around the three characters like the notes

Hamletmaschine,
New York 1986.

of a sonata or the strokes of a cubist painting, with a composite effect of rare intensity. Everything suggesting signs of alarm and perturbation results in verbal information or silent action: a broken tree branch bursts through a window during a storm, the columns of the room are sucked up into the ceiling, shoes are thrown by the three characters as if they were bowling balls falling like lead to the floor with a lacerating sound, an easy chair has for one of its legs the hairy paw of a goat...a female figure then wanders into this empty landscape, invisible to the three characters, while changing her blue costume. Her name is Marianne Kavallierators, and she adds the language of dance to the other languages used in the piece. Evidently, she is the "meek girl," holding a pointed gun as she moves towards the window from which she very slowly lets herself fall. It is not an image from the story, but the reappearance of a dead woman, like the Japanese No, imprinting her calm onto the emotional puzzle.

As with the work in progress in Gibellina, in this concise and very intense show of great purity and strong contagious emotion, where everything relies on the principle of dissociation, Wilson returns to the freshness of his pre-German period, and to inspired perfection, perhaps as a consequence of finally having acquired his own personal atelier at Watermill Center, where the idea for this experiment was born, and which he dedicated to Jerome Robbins. And, in a way, to Madeleine Renaud, the great actress who recently died, and who in *Overture* performed a long solo bent over on all fours, a gesture recaptured and cited in the finale of *The Meek Girl* by Wilson and his excellent colleagues.

Where we discover
that Wilson was Hamlet

"In the beginning was time," we said, initially referring to *Deafman Glance*. We can repeat it at this point, after having reviewed the history and the aesthetics of Bob Wilson and the ways in which he creates rich new ways of interpreting and understanding his project of reinventing the theater. I would like, therefore, to give you a temporary conclusion by way of his first meeting, as an actor, with a character from great theater, who is, unsurprisingly, "the character of all time." My aim is not to peg him, of course, but to look through the rigorous faithfulness to the text that he refuses to interpret, but which he has in fact rewritten, until we find Wilson himself.

Hamlet? For the most recent Robert Wilson this is a dream. Years ago the Texan director produced Heiner Müller's *Hamletmaschine*, like a recollection entangled in a memory device. Now, he doesn't limit himself to producing someone else's version: he plays the role himself in his own original interpretation. He begins on his native soil, in Houston at the Alley Theatre, dedicating enormous lighting and technical expertise to the great text, constructing it around his own solitary presence, reserving for the character the same solo treatment he used with Marianne Hoppe in *Lear*, or for many actors in other literary works. This time, however, the portrait is neither abstract nor objective.

Working on the text with Wolfgang Wiens, Wilson isolated out a script primarily made up of the Prince's lines and some short citations from other characters, especially Hamlet's mother and Ophelia, both of whom are represented by costumes worn by the actor himself. The character revisits these perhaps not-imaginary figures as part of his own dream-like universe, populated exclusively by psychological projections. The play begins with a flashback to a dying Hamlet, laying on top of a pile of large black slabs. Each time he reenters the scene (always dressed in black, but wearing different hats, which every once in a while he ironically lifts off in a music-hall gesture), this mountain stratified by geological anxieties loses some of its pieces, which are of various sizes. The last piece becomes Hamlet's mother's bed—and this is significant, as his anxiety reveals to us—placed in front of a screen against a background filled with changing shades of color. Hamlet reappears in mid-air immersed in blue, on yet another large slab suspended above the stage, to recite the decisive monologue on the bestiality of the human condition, condemning violence, while he plans the inevitable, yet vain, revenge.

The actor ignores all that took place in the court in his absence, and he also practically omits Horatio. He comes to life again during the performance of the play at court, where a scepter appears, dressed up as a puppet, representing the ghost of Hamlet's father. He dramatically repeats the scene of the killing of Polonius in his mother's bedroom three times, each time salvaging a glove, a pair of boots, a medal. The objects count: from the prop trunk before his final exit, costumes are removed to function as images of the many dead characters, laid out in a row as in a wax museum, and then thrown to the wind like ashes. Hamlet's mother and Ophelia are there once again, in the form of pieces of fabric or insignificant recollections that should be lost.

Robert Wilson in
HAMLET: a monologue, 1995.

One man, seated in the desert, is filled with visions of *Hamlet, a monologue*, among the threatening noises of the soundtrack, accompanied by a distant echo of music by Hans Peter Kuhn. Wilson does an extraordinary job as he totally takes possession of the character who, laying down on the stage in the foreground in the position of a dead man, recites his "To be or not to be" to the sky above in a singular moment of truth. He exalts himself like an epileptic in crisis at the thought of action; to the first limits of madness he adds homosexual provocation, brandishing his sword like a penis. He enters and exits, transforming himself, dancing and playing with a fantasy so amusing that it crosses the confines of desperation, while beyond the stage, in this culmination of the 1990s, we see a gallery of his theater history up to the present moment; that is, up to the conquest of an authentic personal dimension of suffering.

ROBERT WILSON THEATER

DEAFMAN GLANCE

Premiered on December 15 and 16, 1970, at the University Theater, University of Iowa, Iowa City. It was presented by the Byrd Hoffman School of Byrds in association with the Center for New Performing Arts, University of Iowa. Subsequent performances were in Brooklyn, New York; Nancy, France; Rome; Paris; and Amsterdam.

Directed by Robert Wilson; music by Alan Lloyd, Igor Demjen et al; scenery by Fred Kolouch (now Kolo) and Robert Wilson; lighting by Richard Nelson in Iowa, Johnny Dodd in New York, and Laurie Lowrie in Europe; costumes by John D'Arcangelo; film components by Franklin Miller.

The cast was comprised of members of the Byrd Hoffman School of Byrds including Wilson, Raymond Andrews, Sheryl Sutton, Andrew de Groat, Igor Demjen, Cindy Lubar, James Neu, Carol Mullins, Mary Peer, Jerome Robbins (in Paris), Susan Sheehy, Scotty Snyder, Stefan Brecht et al.

Received the Drama Desk Award of 1970 for outstanding direction and the Prix de la Critique Française for best foreign play.

KA MOUNTAIN AND GUARDenia TERRACE

a story about a family and some people changing

Premiered on September 2–9, 1972 as one continuous performance beginning at midnight on September 2 and lasting over 168 hours. The performance took place on Haft Tan Mountain near Shiraz, Iran. It was presented by the Byrd Hoffman School of Byrds and the Shiraz-Persepolis Festival of the Arts.

Directed by Robert Wilson, Andrew de Groat, Cindy Lubar, James Neu, Ann Wilson, Mel Andringa, S. K. Dunn et al.; written by Robert Wilson, Andrew de Groat, Jessie Dunn Gilbert, Kikuo Saito, Cindy Lubar, Susan Sheehy, and Ann Wilson; sound composition by Igor Demjen; scenery by Robert Wilson, Mel Andringa, Kikuo Saito, Ann Wilson; costumes by John D'Arcangelo.

The cast was comprised of the members of the Byrd Hoffman School of Byrds.

OVERTURE (PARIS)

Overture for *KA MOUNTAIN AND GUARDenia TERRACE: a story about a family and some people changing* (a two-part presentation lasting seven days)

Part one, gallery presentation:

Opened on November 6, 1972, continuing through November 11, 1972, twelve hours a day, noon to midnight. Presented at the Musée Galliéra by the Festival d'Automne and the Théâtre des Nations.

The exhibition was comprised of works of art by members of the Byrd Hoffman School of Byrds and was contained in seven rooms plus a central hall where the *Overture Chair* was located on a low pedestal in a pool of water. A number of performances took place during the six-day exhibition.

Part two, theater presentation, CYNDI

Premiered on November 11, 1972 at the Opéra Comique, Paris, and lasted for twenty-four hours from midnight to midnight. Presented by the Festival d'Automne and the Théâtre des Nations.

Directed by Robert Wilson; written by Robert Wilson, Cindy Lubar and Ann Wilson; music and sound composition by Igor Demjen; dance by Andrew de Groat; scenery by Paul Thek; costumes by John D'Arcangelo.

The cast included Robert Wilson, Cindy Lubar, Sheryl Sutton, Madeleine Renaud, Edwin Denby, James Neu, Carol Mullins, Scotty Snyder, Andrew de Groat, Ann Wilson, Stefan Brecht et al.

DIA LOG/A MAD MAN A MAD GIANT
A MAD DOG A MAD URGE A MAD FACE

Premiered March 3, 1974, during Contemporanea, Villa Borghese, Rome. Subsequent performances were in Washington D.C.; Shiraz, Iran; and Milan.

A collaborative performance by Robert Wilson and Christopher Knowles. Each presentation was a different configuration of scenic elements, spatial configurations, and participants. In Rome and Shiraz, Wilson and Knowles were joined by Ladan Chidani; in Washington by Robyn Brentano, Jessie Dunn-Gilbert, Carol Mullins, and Ann Wilson; in Milan by Andrew de Groat and Michael Galasso. Various elements from *A Letter for Queen Victoria* were incorporated into the performances.

A LETTER FOR QUEEN VICTORIA

Premiered June 15–22, 1974, at the Teatro Caio Melisso, Spoleto, Italy. It was presented by the xvii Festival Dei Due Mondi. Subsequent performances were in La Rochelle, France; Belgrade; Paris; Zurich; Thonon-les-Bains, Sochaux-Doubs, Mulhouse, Lyon, and Nice, France; and New York City.

Written and directed by Robert Wilson; music by Alan Lloyd with Michael Galasso; additional texts by Christopher Knowles, Cindy Lubar, Stefan Brecht, James Neu; translations by Ann Metelli; choreography by Andrew de Groat; scenery, lighting, and costumes by Fred Kolo and Robert Wilson; slides by Francie Brooks and Kathryn Kean; musical direction by Michael Galasso. Scenery and costume supervision in New York were attributed to Peter Harvey and lighting supervision to Beverly Emmons.

The cast included Sheryl Sutton, Cindy Lubar, Stefan Brecht, Kathryn Cation, Christopher Knowles, Carol Mullins, James Neu, Scotty Snyder, Robert Wilson, Andrew de Groat, Julia Busto et al.

Received the Maharam Award of 1975 for best set design and a Tony nomination for best score and lyrics by Alan Lloyd and Robert Wilson.

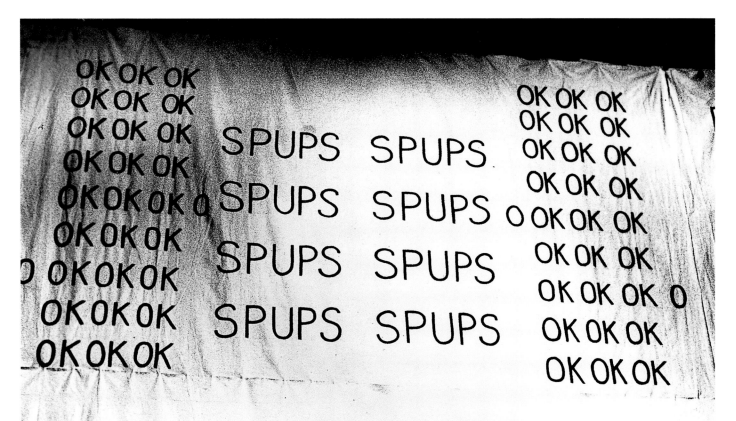

EINSTEIN ON THE BEACH

Premiered July 25–29, 1976, in Avignon, France. Presented by the Byrd Hoffman Foundation, in association with the Festival d'Avignon, Festival d'Automne, Venice Biennale, and the Region of Lombardy. Subsequent performances were in Venice; Belgrade; Brussels; Paris; Hamburg; Rotterdam; Amsterdam; and New York City. Numerous later revivals.

Designed and directed by Robert Wilson; music by Philip Glass; additional texts by Christopher Knowles, Samuel M. Johnson, and Lucinda Childs; choreography by Andrew de Groat; lighting by Beverly Emmons; costumes by D'Arcangelo-Mayer, Paris; audio engineer: Kurt Munkacsi; stage manager: Julia Gillette.

The cast included Lucinda Childs, Sheryl Sutton, Samuel M. Johnson, Andrew de Groat, Robert Wilson et al. Music performed by the Philip Glass Ensemble.

Awards included the Prix de la Critique du Syndicat de la Critique à Paris, Grand Prize at the Belgrade Festival, and the Lumen Award of 1977 for lighting design.

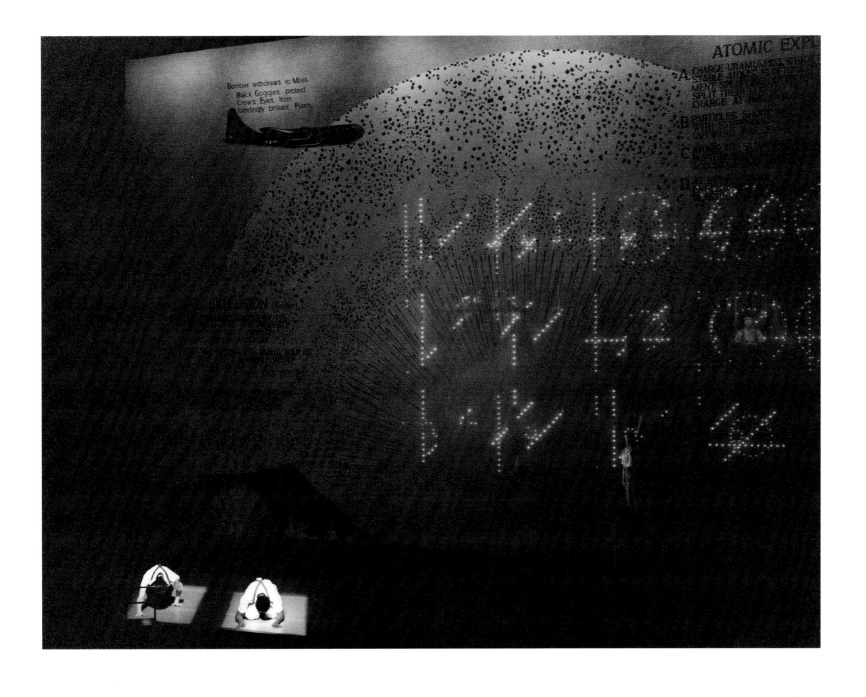

I WAS SITTING ON MY PATIO THIS GUY APPEARED I THOUGHT I WAS HALLUCINATING

Premiered April 2 and 3, 1977, at the Quirk Auditorium, Eastern Michigan University, Ypsilanti. Produced by Richard Barr. Subsequent performances were in Philadelphia; Austin, Clear Lake City, and Dallas, Texas; Los Angeles; San Francisco; St. Paul, Minnesota; New York City; Paris; Rotterdam; The Hague; Amsterdam; Zurich; Geneva; Milan; Berlin; Stuttgart; and London.

Co-directed by Robert Wilson and Lucinda Childs; music by Alan Lloyd; scenery by Robert Wilson and Christina Giannini; lighting by Beverly Emmons; costumes by Arnold Scaasi; film by Greta Wing Miller; production manager: Robert LoBianco.

The cast included Robert Wilson and Lucinda Childs.

I WAS SITTING ON MY PATIO THIS GUY APPEARED I THOUGHT I WAS HALLUCINATING

DEATH DESTRUCTION AND DETROIT

Premiered February 12, 1979, at the Schaubühne am Halleschen Ufer, Berlin. Subsequent performances were at the Berlin Theatertreffen.

Designed and directed by Robert Wilson; music by Alan Lloyd, with additional material by Keith Jarrett and Randy Newman; German translation: Peter Krumme and Bernd Samland; additional texts by Maita di Niscemi; scenic collaborator: Manfred Dittrich; lighting by Beverly Emmons and Renato Berta; costumes by Moidele Bickel; sound design by Hans Peter Kuhn.

The cast included Sabine Andreas, Philippe Chemin, Christine Oesterline, Otto Sander, Gernd Wameling, Günther Ehlert et al.

Received German Press Prize for a new play.

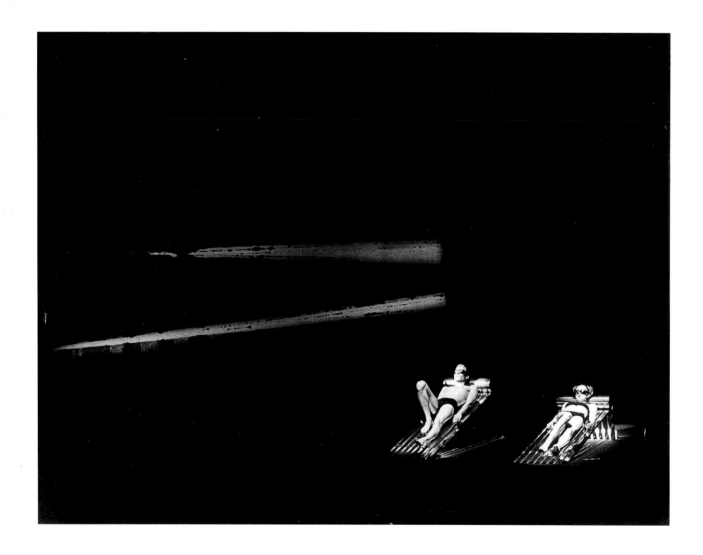

EDISON

Premiered on October 9–13, 1979. at the Théâtre National Populaire, Villeurbanne (Lyon), France. A co-production of Byrd Hoffman Foundation and TNP. Subsequent performances were in Milan and Paris.

Directed and designed by Robert Wilson; additional dialogue and research by Maita di Niscemi; translation by Philippe Chemin; music by Michael Riesman with Gottschalk, Miles Davis, Puccini, Scarlatti, etc.; music director: Tania León; scenery by Robert Wilson and Tom Woodruff; lighting by André Diot and Robert LoBianco; costumes by Jacques Schmidt; sound by Jacob Burckhardt and André Serré. Original film sequence by Thomas Alva Edison.

The cast included Susan Berman, Randy Buck, Philippe Chemin, Ralph Douglas, Isabel Eberstadt, John Erdman, Sandra Johnson; Terrell Robinson, Joniruth White.

THE GOLDEN WINDOWS
DIE GOLDENEN FENSTER

Premiered on May 29, 1982, at the Münchner Kammerspiele, Munich. Subsequent performances were in Vienna and New York City.

Direction, design, costumes, and lighting by Robert Wilson; music by Tania León, Gavin Bryars, and J. C. Pepusch; dramaturgy and translation by Michael Wachsmann; lighting by Markus Bönzli; costumes by Christophe de Menil; sound design by Hans Peter Kuhn.

The cast included Peter Lühr, Maria Nicklisch, Edgar Selge, and Irene Clarin.

Received Der Rosenstrauss, Tage Zeitung, in 1982.

the CIVIL warS:
a tree is best measured when it is down

Dutch section: premiere, Rotterdam 1983 [photos on pages 116–117]

German section: Act I, scene a; Act III, scene e; Act IV

Premiered on January 19, 1984, at the Köln Schauspielhaus, Cologne. Co-produced by Köln Schauspielhaus and WDR radio. Subsequent performances at the Berlin Theaterreffen plus American production in 1985.

Direction, design and lighting by Robert Wilson; collaborator and co-author: Heiner Müller; music by Philip Glass, David Byrne, Hans Peter Kuhn, Frederick the Great, Thomas Tallis, and Franz Schubert; dramaturg: Wolfgang Wiens; scenic assistant: Regine Friese; lighting by Franz-Peter David and Heinrich Brunke; costumes by Yoshio Yabara; sound design by Hans Peter Kuhn; film by Edgardo Cozarinsky and Hella Viezke.

The cast included Ingrid Andree, Anna Henkel, Fred Hospowsky, Hannelore Lübeck, Georg Peter-Pilz, Rainer Philippi, Ilse Ritter et al.

Italian section: Prologue and Act V

Premiered March 26, 1984, at the Teatro dell'Opera in Rome. Subsequent performances were given in Scheveningen, Utrecht, Eindhoven, and Amsterdam, the Netherlands. Presented by the Netherlands Opera. A 1986 production featured new choreography by Ulysses Dove and a duet for Hercules and Alcmena by Philip Glass and Maita di Niscemi. Presented by the Brooklyn Academy of Music.

Directed by Robert Wilson; music by Philip Glass; text by Maita di Niscemi and Robert Wilson; choreography by Jim Self; music director: Marcello Panni; choral director: Gianni Lazzari; scenery by Tom Kamm and Robert Wilson; lighting by Beverly Emmons; costumes by Christophe de Menil; sound design by Hans Peter Kuhn.

The cast included Seta del Grande, Ruby Hinds, Luigi Petroni, Franco Leschig, Jim Self et al.

THE KNEE PLAYS

the CIVIL warS: a tree is best measured when it is down

The American section: The Knee Plays

Premiered on April 25–28, 1984, at Walker Art Center, Minneapolis. Presented by Walker Art Center in association with the Guthrie Theater. Subsequent performances have been in Frankfurt; Bobigny, France; Madrid; Venice; Bologne; Cologne; Cambridge, Massachusetts; Los Angeles; Berkeley; Boulder, Colorado; Albuquerque, New Mexico; Detroit; Washington DC; New York City; Burlington, Vermont; Austin and Houston Texas; Chicago; Tokyo; and Brisbane, Australia.

Direction and scenery by Robert Wilson; music and words by David Byrne; artistic assistance by Adelle Lutz; choreography by Suzushi Hanayagi; design by Robert Wilson, David Byrne, and Jun Matsuno; lighting by Robert Wilson and Julie Archer.

The cast included David Byrne (narration), Donald Byrd, Maria Cheng, Frank Conversano, Gail Donneirfeld, Denise Gustafson, Marilyn Habermas-Scher, Suzushi Hanayagi, Cho Kyoo-Hyun, Satoru Shimizaki.

Received the Bessie Award (New York) of 1987 for dance.

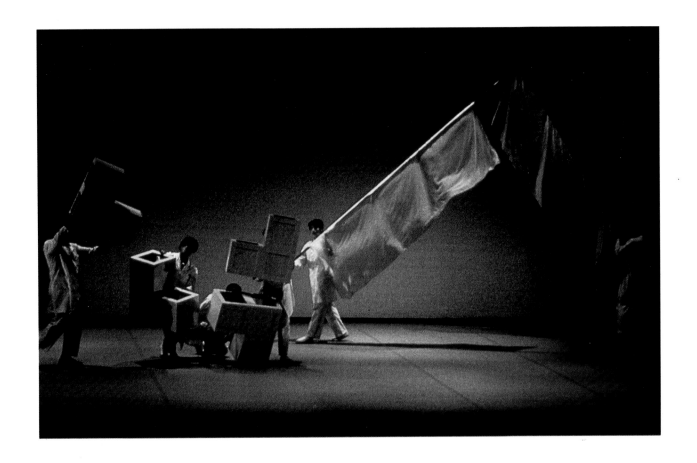

ALCESTIS

Premiered March 12–23 (previews March 7–11), 1986, at the Loeb Drama Center, Cambridge, Massachusetts. Presented by the American Repertory Theater. Subsequent performances were in Bobigny, France. The German production premiered on April 19, 1988, at the Württemberg State Theater, Stuttgart.

Adapted by Robert Wilson from the play by Euripides; additional texts: *Description of a Picture* (Prologue) by Heiner Müller, translated by Carl Weber, and the Japanese kyogen, *The Birdcatcher in Hell* (Epilogue), translated by Mark Oshima. (Excerpts from Rainer Maria Rilke's poem, "Alkestis" were incorporated into the main text.) Concept, direction, and design by Robert Wilson; music by Laurie Anderson; movement construction by Suzushi Hanayagi; scenery by Tom Kamm and Robert Wilson; lighting by Jennifer Tipton and Robert Wilson; costumes by John Conklin; sound design by Hans Peter Kuhn.

The cast included Eric D. Menyuk, Rodney Hudson, Diane D'Aquila, Paul Rudd (Ken Howard in Bobigny), Harry S. Murphy, Jeremy Geidt, Thomas Derrah, John Bottoms.

German production:

Translation by Kriederike Roth and Ann-Christian Rommen; dramaturg: Ellen Hammer; lighting by Robert Wilson, Uwe Belzner, and Jennifer Tipton; costumes by Joachim Herzog and John Conklin.

The cast included Thomas Goritzki, Sheryl Sutton, Anne Beunent, Stephan Bissmeier, Michael Mendl, Klaus Steiger et al.

HAMLETMASCHINE

German Production

Premiered October 4 through November 30, 1986 (with later performances on April 16–23, 1987) at the Theater in der Kunsthalle, Hamburg. A co-production of the Thalia Theater and Hochschule fur Musik und Darstellende Kunst. Subsequent performances were in Berlin.

Direction and design by Robert Wilson; music by Jerry Leiber and Mike Stoller; dramaturg: Wolfgang Wiens; lighting by Jennifer Tipton and Robert Wilson; sound design by Peter J. Stoller.

DEATH DESTRUCTION & DETROIT II

Premiered February 27 through July 4, 1987, at the Schaubühne am Lehniner Platz, Berlin.

Direction and design by Robert Wilson; texts by Franz Kafka, Heiner Müller, Robert Wilson, Maita di Niscemi, and Cindy Lubar; choreography by Suzushi Hanayagi; dramaturg: Klaus Metzger; lighting by Heinrich Brunke and Robert Wilson; costumes by Moidele Bickel; sound design by Hans Peter Kuhn.

The cast included Libgart Schwarz, Ernst Stötzner, Paul Burian, Gerd Wameling, Udo Samel, Gregor Hansen, Tina Engel, Peter Simonischek, Branko Samarouski, Elke Petri, Christine Oesterlein, Jezy Milton, Matthias Matuschka, Lucia Hartpeng et al.

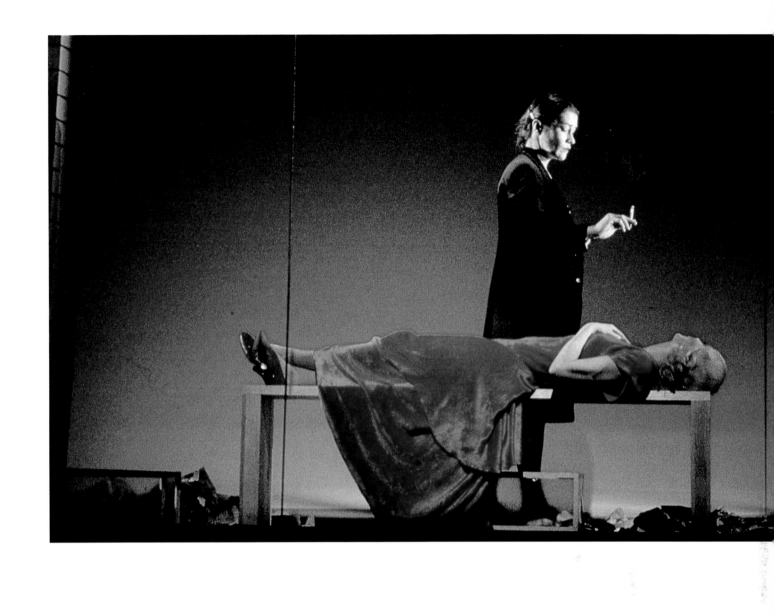

LE MARTYRE DE SAINT SÉBASTIEN

Premiered March 23–26, March 28–31, and April 7–9, April 11–16, 1988. Production commissioned by Rudolf Nurejev for the Ballet de l'Opéra de Paris. Created in Bobigny, France at the Maison de la Culture MC93. Subsequent performances were in New York City and Paris.

Directed and designed by Robert Wilson; based on the text by Gabriele D'Annunzio with music by Claude Debussy; choreography by Suzushi Hanayagi and Robert Wilson; dramaturg: Ellen Hammer; scenery by Robert Wilson and Xavier de Richemont; lighting by Howell Binkley and Robert Wilson; costumes by Frida Parmeggiani; sound design by Hans Peter Kuhn.

The cast included the Ballet de l'Opéra de Paris and the Étoiles, Sylvie Guillem, Michael Denard, Patrick Dupond, and the performers Philippe Chemin, Sheryl Sutton.

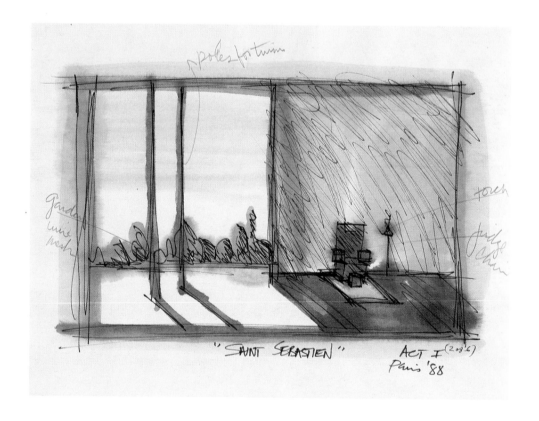

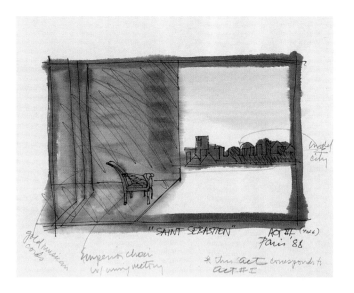

ORLANDO

Premiered on November 21, 1989, at the Schaubühne am Lehniner Platz, Berlin. Subsequent performances have been given in French and English versions.

From the novel by Virginia Woolf; adapted by Robert Wilson and Darryl Pinckney; directed and designed by Robert Wilson; co-directed by Ann-Christin Rommen; music by Hans Peter Kuhn; lighting by Heinrich Brunke and Robert Wilson; dramaturg: Wolfgang Wiens.

The original version was interpreted by Jutta Lampe; the French version by Isabelle Huppert; the English version by Miranda Richardson.

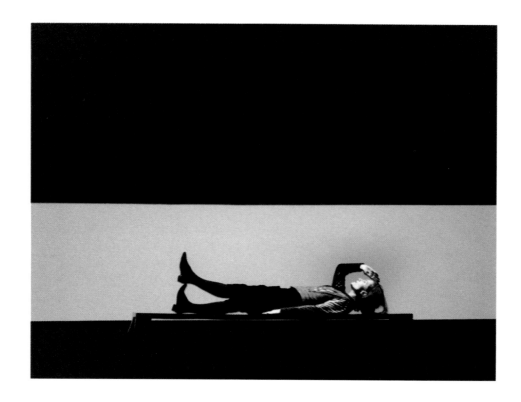

THE BLACK RIDER
the casting of the magic bullets

Premiered on March 31, 1990, at the Thalia theater, Hamburg. Subsequent performances were in Paris, Amsterdam, Berlin, Genoa, Seville, and New York City.

Based on *Der Freischütz* by August Apel and Friedrich Laun, and on *The Fatal Marksman* by Thomas de Quincey; adapted, directed, and designed by Robert Wilson; music and lyrics by Tom Waits; text by William S. Burroughs; dramaturgy and translations: Wolfgang Wiens; costumes by Frida Parmeggiani; lighting by Heinrich Brunke and Robert Wilson; music direction and arrangements by Greg Cohen; sound design by Gerd Bessler.

The cast included Heinz Vossbrink, Dominique Horwitz, Gerd Kunath, Angelika Thomas, Annette Paulmann, Stefan Kurt, Klaus Schreiber, Jörg Holm, Sona Cervena, Monika Tahal, Jan Moritz Steffen, and Susi Eisenkolb.

THE MAGIC FLUTE

Premiered on June 27, 1991, at the Opéra Bastille, Paris.

Music by Wolfgang Amadeus Mozart; directed and designed by Robert Wilson; dramaturg: Ellen Hammer; co-directed by Giuseppe Frigeni; music direction by Armin Jordan, Orchestre et choeurs de l'Opéra de Paris; choreography by Andrew de Groat; lighting by Heinrich Brunke and Robert Wilson; costumes by John Conklin.

The cast included Clarry Bartha, Christian Boesch, Philippe Duminy, Anne Constantin, Cynthia Haymon, Ewa Malas-Godlewska, Luciana Serra, Hél_ne Perraguin, David Rendall, Hanna Schaer, Carsten Stabell, Volker Vogel et al.

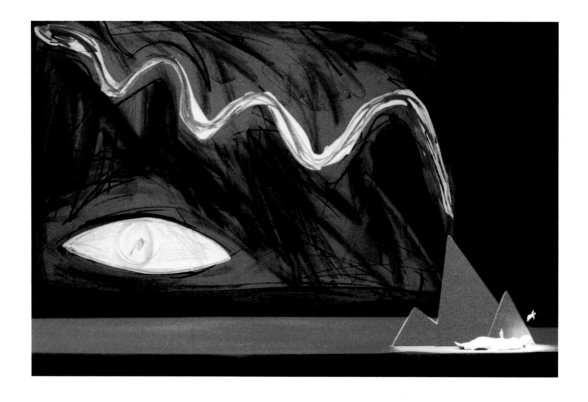

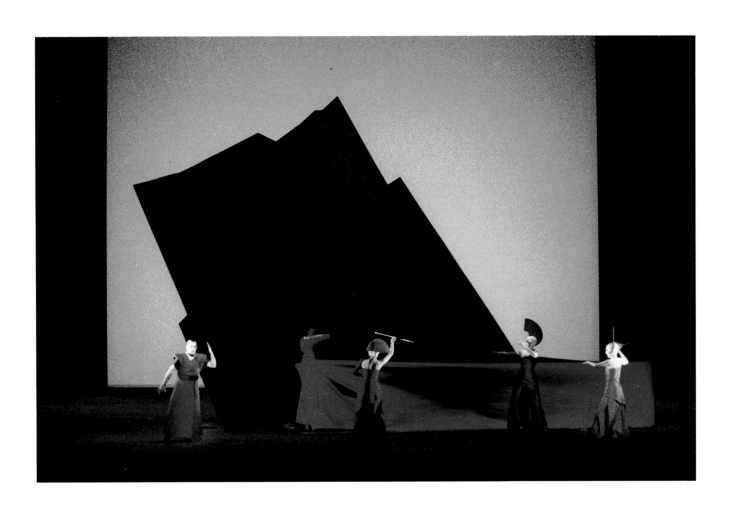

DOCTOR FAUSTUS LIGHTS THE LIGHTS

Premiered April 15, 1992, at the Hebbel Theater, Berlin. Subsequent performances were in Frankfurt; Venice; Rome; New York; Salzburg; Maubeuge, France; Paris; Antwerp; Milan; Montreal; Edinburgh; Lisbon; Budapest; Prague; and Hong Kong.

By Gertrude Stein; directed and designed by Robert Wilson; dramaturg: Peter Krumme; music by Hans Peter Kuhn; costumes by Hans Thiemann; lighting by Heinrich Brunke and Robert Wilson; choreography by Suzushi Hanayagi.

The cast included Matthias Bundschuh, Christian Ebert, Florian Fitz, Katrin Heller, Wiebke Kayser, Thomas Lehmann, Thilo Mandel, Heiko Senst, Moritz Sostmann, Karla Trippel, Gabriele Völsch, and Martin Vogel.

MADAME BUTTERFLY

Premiered on November 19, 1993 at the Opéra Bastille, Paris. Subsequent performances were in Bologna and Paris.

Music by Giacomo Puccini; directed and designed by Robert Wilson; co-directed by Giuseppe Frigeni; dramaturg: Holm Keller; music direction by Myung-Whun Chung; choreography by Suzushi Hanayagi; costumes by Frida Parmeggiani; lighting by Heinrich Brunke and Robert Wilson.

The cast included Nicoletta Curiel, Georges Gautier, Viacheslav Polozov, Dana Soviero, Valentina Sodipov, William Stone et al.

THE MEEK GIRL

Premiered on October 11–23, 1994 at MC93, Bobigny, France. Presented by the Festival d'Automne, Paris. Subsequent performances were in Antwerp; Zurich; Grenoble; Frankfurt; and Caen, France.

Based on a story by Fyodor Dostoyevsky; adapted by Robert Wilson and Wolfgang Wiens [in English, French, German]; directed and designed by Robert Wilson; costumes by Christophe de Menil; lighting by Andreas Fuchs and Robert Wilson; sound design by Stephan Kurt and Gerd Bessler.

The cast included Charles Chemin, Marianna Kavallieratos, Thomas Lehmann, and Robert Wilson.

HAMLET: a monologue

Premiered on May 24, 1995, at the Alley Theatre, Houston. Subsequent performances were in Venice, New York, Paris, Seville, Lisbon, Helsinki, and Vienna.

Based on the play by William Shakespeare; adapted by Wolfgang Wiens and Robert Wilson; directed and designed by Robert Wilson; co-directed by Ann-Christin Rommen; dramaturg: Wolfgang Wiens; music by Hans Peter Kuhn; costumes by Frida Parmeggiani; lighting by Stephen Strawbridge and Robert Wilson.

Robert Wilson, soloist.

173

BLUEBEARD'S CASTLE / ERWARTUNG

Premiered on August 24, 1995 at the Kleines Festspielhaus (Salzburger Festspiele), Salzburg. Subsequent performances were in Zurich (*Bluebeard's Castle* only, paired with *Oedipus Rex*).

By Bela Bartók (*Bluebeard's Castle*) and Arnold Schönberg (*Erwartung*); directed by Robert Wilson; scenes by Robert Wilson and Stephanie Engeln; co-directed by Giuseppe Frigeni; dramaturg: Holm Keller; costumes by Frida Parmeggiani; music direction by Christoph von Dohnányi; lighting by Heinrich Brunke and Robert Wilson.

The cast included Markella Hatziano, Robert Hale (*Bluebeard's Castle*); Jessye Norman (*Erwartung*); and the Vienna Philharmonic.

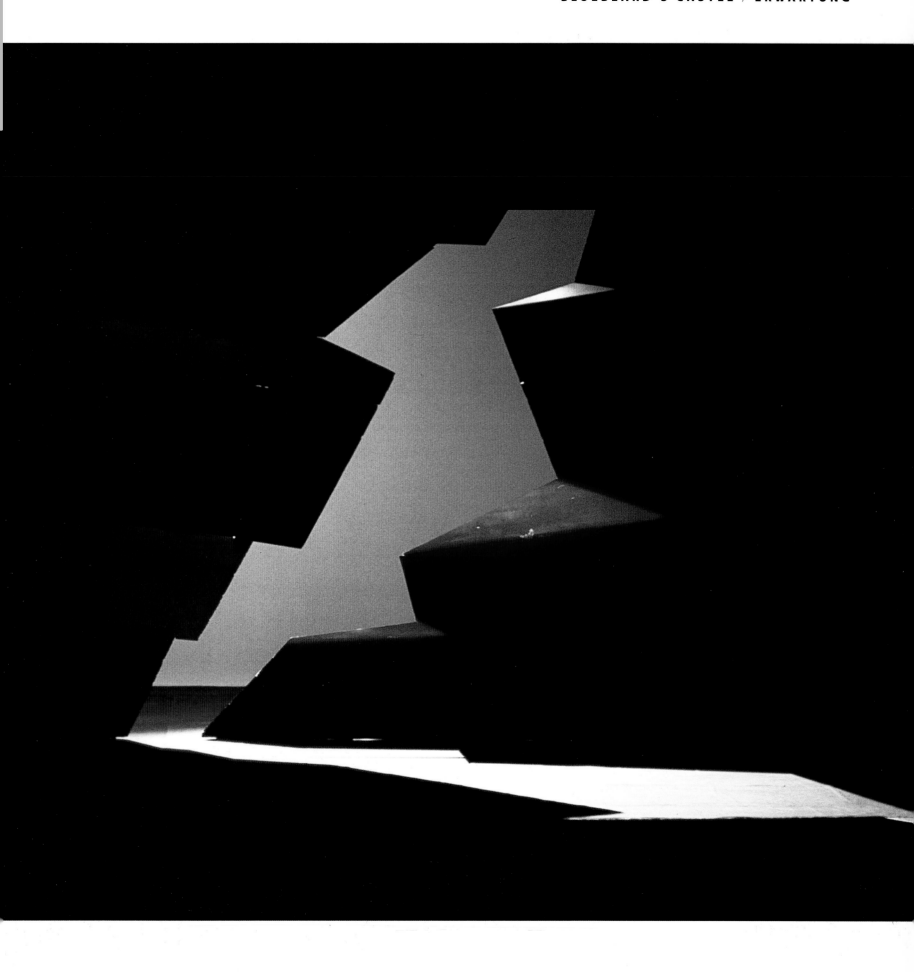

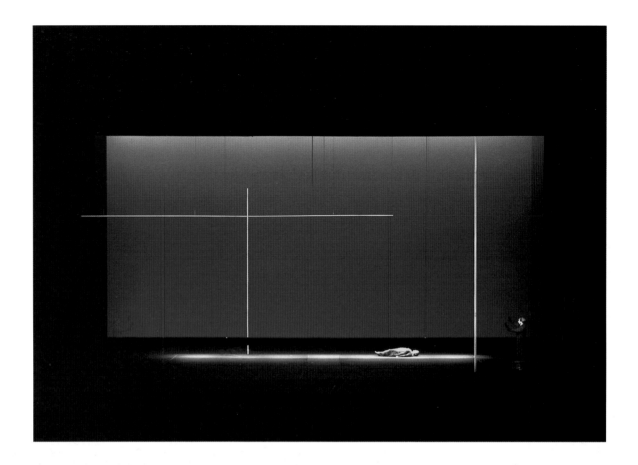

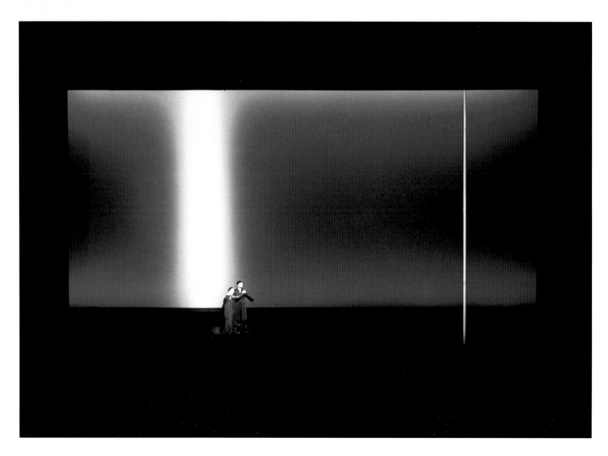

Franco Bertoni

ROBERT WILSON: THEMES AND SYMBOLS OF THE MODERN

Like only a few other figures in twentieth-century art, Robert Wilson has managed to move beyond the expressions of his own particular art form—in his case the theater—to bring into focus and develop a more general language, one that is able to investigate, to interpret, and more significantly, to move very different forms (theater, installation, images and object themselves, even architecture) to great expressiveness.

It would be belittling to confine Wilson to a single specific art, despite the preeminence of theater in his work. This would diminish the importance of his essential contribution to refining an expressive form for our collective end-of-the-millennium sensitivity.

"A la Wilson" or "Wilsonian" has become established as a term in art criticism, in the literary journals, and in design and architecture magazines. In a postscript to Raymond Carver, Fernanda Pivano outlined minimalism: "Starting with John Cage who gave the movement its archetype with his 4'33", it passes through the dance of Yvonne Rainer, Lucinda Childs and Trisha Brown and the compositions of LaMonte Young and Morton Feldman, to arrive at *the CIVIL warS* by Bob Wilson with the music of Philip Glass."[1] Wilson's work is also repeatedly published and cited in the international press as indispensable to any discussion of minimalism. Among these sources, in reference to the 1993 Biennale in Venice,[2] and to 1990s design, *Memory/Loss* is referred to as a work that introduces the new minimalism of these years. These sources further add that if a difference exists "between artistic minimalism ... and that which we see blossoming now, it is perhaps in a more 'vital energy' which joins a few significant events of the art world *(Memory/Loss)* to the most truly expressive objects of recent design." It is clear from this and from other examples that Wilson's *oeuvre* in a number of fields is considered representative of recent developments. Various industrial firms have even tried to manufacture some of the objects Wilson makes (chairs and tables) for his theater pieces.

This is an indication of the vitality of a path taken, of a way of thinking, and of working methods which magnificently have been able to bring together an enormous number of complex tendencies, influences, and artistic events (theater, painting, sculpture, design, literature, music) into a crystal clear synthesis of stainless simplicity.

In this highly developed Western world on the edge of disintegration, a world of idiotic babble, meaninglessness aggravated by strife and hopelessness, Wilson's work is a product of the sudden reawakening of the American Dream: to be oneself again in space and time, through simplicity enriched with echoes and memories,

Parsifal, act I, 1985.
Drawing.

with silence, and with a stillness in which nothing at all seems to happen. He has become justly famous, while his work has had a profound and lasting effect.

By repeatedly distilling artistic currents and the various artistic mediums which have been used to analyze our unease–our inarticulations, our tiredness before the problems of life, before every sort of violence, our own falseness–Wilson has been able to suggest a new balance. He purifies in his illusory but authentic world the crudeness of matter, sees everything once again with the innocence of children and mad people, and gives us back–free of convention and restrictions–a vision of our everyday experience.

It is not easy to single out, from the complex sources of inspiration and the multi-faceted products of Wilson's creativity, even a few keys to understanding his dream world. He has used a vast number of forms of expression: from non-objective suprematism to dada, from Marcel Duchamp to surrealism, from pop art to minimalism, from found-object to advanced technology. Among the constants, however, is an ethical sense, a model of behavior, a vision of a particular world, one that is certainly submerged in the collective awareness as the century ends.

Wilson's ruthless borrowing from so many sources is perhaps a reflection of how immobility can be used to escape present surroundings, into time, space, and memory, through work which seeks life. In doing this, as John Cage put it, "Art becomes a sort of experiment with which one experiments life."

The same apparent incoherence governs Wilson's staging, where movements, sounds, and gestures have no reference to narration or description. Often, instead, they are characterized by a lack of any logic, by dissonance, symbolizing the necessity in life to experiment, to move forward with jumps, to throw out any argument that seems reasonable and coherent, to proceed without ever understanding exact limits.

It would not be wrong to claim that Wilson's "anthropology" is a symbolic one, in the sense that he places man in a vast, even cosmic context, where man belongs and where man is also the symbolic image.

The enormous need for image and symbols is well known from sociological and ethnic evidence throughout history. It reappears over and over again, always with similarities which cannot possibly be related only to their

The Magical Flute, act II,
scene XIX, 1991. Drawing.

time or place, or to any cultural or racial ties. It is important to note that this need has nothing to do with some well-worn older step on the ladder of man's progress. Rather, as Mircea Eliade writes, "symbolic thought doesn't belong only to children, to poets and mad people; it precedes language and narrative logic, to show those sides of reality which are the most revealing, ones which would otherwise escape any other means of description."[3]

The preeminence of this symbolic view over that of thought is a recent reality in Western society, a society, weakened and exhausted by materialism, that is trying to avoid the many barriers thrown up between thought and feeling. This is the rediscovery, in fact, of a dimension where each person has a strong sense of belonging to larger realities: spiritual ones, humane ones, and realities that can remember.

Wilson's work has in it certain central themes. Among these are an anti-naturalism, an anti-descriptivism, abstraction, emptiness, silence, duration of time, memory, the use of minimalism to obtain things, and actions, colors, and sounds with a strong anti-psychological quality. The object is to use elements which are not tied directly to normal existence and which, precisely because of this, open the mind and the feelings to new and unexpected hopes.

The representation of the abstract is a crucial concept in modern art. The abstract, the non-objective, is no longer relegated to merely decorative functions, but becomes an eloquent, symbolic form of spiritual needs, of new values, of the symptoms of discomfort with reality.

Kandinsky defined this as "an overthrowing of values, the slow abandonment of the exterior, and an equally slow turning towards the interior."[4] This is done through a restricted geometric or elementary vocabulary where "color is the key, the eye the little hammer which strikes it, and the soul is an instrument of numberless chords." That was the first concrete step in a journey which, unlike others in this century, continues today. Presumably the journey will take on new force and meaning as materialism develops between our faith in progress, and a grim outlook for its future.

It is worth noting that as early as 1907, W. Worringer wrote something that influenced a large part of modern art.[5] Although his view was not exceptional, he was still among the first to be aware of the effects of psycho-

The Magic Flute, act I, scenes XV and VI, 1991. Drawings.

analytical thought, how it was fundamental to the history of civilization, and how in an even greater way it was essential to the art of the first years of the twentieth century.

Worringer understood that there is a link between a tendency towards abstraction, and expressions of distress: "What are the psychic premises which spur abstraction? Whereas a tendency towards empathy is produced by a happy relationship of pantheistic trust between man and the phenomena of the exterior world, a tendency towards abstraction is caused by the inner uneasiness which man may feel before these phenomena, which corresponds on a religious level to a strong tendency towards the transcendental."

As in agoraphobia, which describes a person's fear of open spaces because of an unsureness of his or her own physical and psychic force, the distress which Worringer touches upon is one of the great illnesses of the century: a sense of inanition "when faced with the vast, incoherent, and baffling world of exterior things" (real as well as social).

In such a state of serious unease, the incentive for art has little consistency. So, one hopes to achieve "a self-projection into objects of the external world, and through these to take pleasure in oneself … isolate the simple object from its arbitrariness and apparent sources, making it immortal by putting it next to abstract forms, and so find a quiet place, a refuge in the disappearance of phenomena. The real hope is, so to speak, to tear the object out of its natural surroundings, out of the flow of existence, to free it from everything in it that depends on life … to make it essential and unchangeable, to take it near to its absolute value."

These comments were decisive for the birth of abstraction in twentieth-century art and, as we shall see, also for minimalism. They were also decisive for certain basic ideas in Wilson's work.

Worringer goes on to outline his thesis: "… a simple line, drawn straight, should offer man, distressed by darkness and by a confusion of phenomena, enormous happiness. When the last residual instinct that has a link with life, and the dependence on that instinct are gone, there will exist the most absolute form; pure abstraction … this is a law, even a necessity…. But there is no object in nature that can serve as a model for such abstraction

The Magic Flute, 1991.

Lohengrin, 1991.
Model.

… so abstract straight lines are the only and the highest forms in which man can find peace, when faced with the confused picture which the world offers."

Worringer's meaning is particularly important in the context of a whole series of things which unite this need for abstraction with the symptom of unease. It was Kasimir Malevich, one of the first painters of the abstract movement, who began to bring about this union.

Malevich stands out clearly in those early years, both because of his radical art, and because of his deeply thoughtful theories. His *Black Square,* a famous canvas of 1913, depicts a large monochrome square. Malevich takes painting to point zero, to a place where there are no associations whatsoever with objectivity or psychology. A painting is only a painting. The painted square is only a painted square.

Malevich's choice of elementary geometry was induced by a reality where we do not recognize ourselves, and from a need to transcend the world of things, to arrive at a non-objective reality through which the world can be remade.

Malevich discovered that objectiveness is only one existing arrangement among others: a mere possibility, not an absolute historical reality.

Objectiveness, for Malevich, is a finalistic process which assumes that the means are an end, and which excludes any attempt to go beyond the limits of the means. Conversely, he claimed that life is non-objective when it manages to go beyond the world of conventions, the obvious world, which has no values. His simple, absolute, silent black square makes no reference to a life of objects, but rather primes a release mechanism of unconscious emotions. The square turns into a symbol of a tormented part of being, of the nothingness and the irreality of the world of objective representation. At the same time, it is also a symbol for the majesty and reality of all that is not. This is a suggestion for a means of existence in which art is a real thing, in contrast with other unreal ways humans behave, which are substantially valueless.

With Malevich we see two sides to the artist who, like a "blade runner," turns to abstraction as a means of communication. On the one hand, he does this for a very simple and reassuring reconstruction of the world; on the other hand this expresses an almost Kafka-esque tragedy of the absurd: "The entire universe moves in the vortex of non-objective emotion. Even man goes forward carrying his whole object-filled world, in the infinity of the non-objective, so that all his apparent things are really non-objects because they are not of any essentiality. It follows therefore that the practical 'reality' of objects is not real at all."[6]

Malevich's uncompromising tone is sometimes more convincing to modern sensibilities when he manages to bring together the value of abstraction, of emotion, of the sentimental element, and therefore of the non-objective, in nature's forms: "It is true that we become passionate before the beauty of hills, of rivers, of spring and autumn with golden colors. But does this mean that all natural phenomena are based on laws of beauty? Does the sun set according to these principles? The edges of clouds color themselves thanks to an artistic attitude? Cannot the hills, valleys and gorges, which so excite us, be produced by things being churned up and by changes in equilibrium rather than being the fruit of aesthetic laws? This law of beauty can not even be found in the work of the artist because all he does is put new order into things which are already there. Whence does the artist get the beauty with which to express his own work, if all the elements which he uses are subject to natural laws, so that he is limited to merely arranging them in some new way, according to differences of composition and weight? In the same way, even wisdom does not exist in nature, nor those last (ultimate) causes which man wants to know at any cost.

If truth exists, it exists only in non-objectivity, in nothing less."

And more: "Nature functions without meaning or ends, and shows herself to us without reason or logic."

The importance of Malevich's art and of his theoretical ideas has been noted in art criticism. What is interesting is to connect the isolation and emancipation of abstract communicative forms based on geometric elements, with a state of unease, with an incapacity or lack of willingness to have any relationship with the real world. The real world is rejected in favor of a state of being which has been totally cut off from any relationship with it.

It is only by doing this that one is able to find new forms of mental and emotional freedom.

This way of looking at things sees society itself as the basic problem, and the overcoming of this mistaken way of seeing as the object.

It is interesting to note how already in 1913 Malevich–aware perhaps that for his vision to be expressed correctly a more involved medium was needed–had painted his black square into scenery for Krucenich's *Victory Over the Sun*. But he painted its geometric elements next to it. Over the passage of time, these became symbols of suprematist painting. This is a surprising anticipation of some of Robert Wilson's preparative work, in which geometric elements also take on fundamental importance: from his luminous rectangle of *Einstein on the Beach* to the geometries of *Orlando*, to the superimposition of squares and rectangles in *Lohengrin*.

Malevich's effort to move beyond the objective world, even if the effort was systemless and confused, and surrounded by a questionable halo of mysticism, still seems a fundamentally important step in the history of

Orlando, intermezzo 2/3, 1989. Drawing.

Orlando, part I, 1989. Drawing.

I Was Sitting On My Patio…, 1977. Drawing.

artistic thought. Also, in its radicalness and foresight it was a forerunner of much that happened after the Second World War in the United States: minimalism, land art, and *arte povera* all found their strong points in the negation of a society whose values were subordinated to appearances, to the exterior of things, and to commerce.

Another phrase from Malevich: "non-objective perceptions form the content of my painting: these put me in harmony with the All," points to another of the salient symbols of this artistic creed. It acknowledges the need for some greater entity with which to explain our existence, give sense to our actions, and against which to measure our efforts—something beyond our ordinary everyday world.

The "All" of Malevich corresponds to the "Emptiness" of the minimalists: that unlimited, suspended place where alone can take place a true meeting that has not been corrupted by false values—a meeting between the human being and things, between one human being and another (between the actors and the objects on a stage, between the actors and the spectators).

Central to Taoist ontology and present in Oriental thought since the *Book of Changes*, the idea of emptiness also becomes important in Western artistic thought from John Cage to Barnett Newman. Cage's experimental work and Newman's pictures—like *Vir Heroicus Sublimicus* of 1950–51, in which a large red ground is crossed only by five vertical lines, which make it read not only spatially but also physically/temporally—become the incunabula for the formation of many generations of American and European artists.

The stylistic austerity of the minimalists unquestionably has a foundation in the theoretical works of Malevich, but its stronger *raison d'être* lies in its reaction to the vitality and powerful expressiveness of gestural art, and to the excesses of American materialism and commercialism, seen so clearly later in the supermarket of pop art.

Spiritual tension and "political" zeal take artists like Robert Morris, Donald Judd, Carl Andre, Bruce Nauman, and Dan Flavin towards the austere, ascetic atmosphere which distinguishes minimalist poetry. This is a strongly modernist view, which presumes that thought and action can still change a concept and a way of life.

"For me, minimal means maximum economy to achieve maximum objectives" (Carl Andre).

For years, Barnett Newman and Mark Rothko were on this road. In fact, in a statement of intent sent to the editor of the *New York Times* in 1943, the latter wrote: "We believe in the simple statement for complex thought … for us, art is an adventure in an unknown world. The world of imagination is without illusions and is strongly opposed to anything practical."

One can see in these pictures that the active function of the void is the opposite of a no man's land. It is precisely the void, the calculated absence of the excess of its opposite—which is all filled up with sounds, colors, forms—that permits an exceptional but never excessive investigative process of interiorization and transformation. Both the object and perception undergo radical changes. We discover that the "Void" is not something which does not exist, but is, on the contrary, highly expressive.

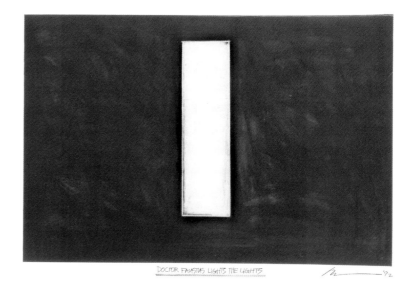

Doctor Faustus Lights
the Lights, act III, scene I,
1992. Drawing.

It is well known in Chinese and Japanese painting that the "empty" part of a picture can occupy as much as two thirds of the canvas, and that this is very important to the whole representation and the way it is seen. Of this Wilson is certainly aware. He has been attracted by Zen philosophy, as well as by the attention in No theater to sounds and to ritual gestures, the horizontal and vertical planes representing respectively time and space. These are forms which Wilson inverts on stage, where he uses the plane of the stage to represent space, while its depth becomes a symbol of timing.

Wilson's scenes, stage arrangements, and images are all permeated by this sense of the void, of the clear presence of a bigger field, which includes both the visible and the illusionistic realities of the theater.

But this void of Wilson's is actually alive with hidden meanings. It is bits and pieces of things given hidden senses, a place where the human figure, where every object, every light appears as a voice which has not yet been understood, its sounds still hanging in the air. Every color, every action, every form has innumerable echoes and resonances. In Wilson's emptiness, myriad things listen to each other and to themselves in grand conversation, sometimes secret and quiet, sometimes clear and loud.

How can one forget the scores of characters, objects, movements (the ostriches, the tortoises, which held up the stage, the angel, the flying chair, the house, the palm) in *Deafman Glance;* the miraculous sky in *Die Goldenen Fenster;* scene C of the first act of *the CIVIL warS,* with the grid, the trellis-work, the mountains, and the two enormous giraffes; the expressionistic dreaminess of *The Black Rider.*

"Black A, white E, red I, green U, blue O ..." wrote the "prophet" Rimbaud, making it clear that this is possible only after a necessary and inevitable total cleansing of the mind and the senses.

The "Void"–liberation from the oppression and the mental and physical conditioning brought about by matter–becomes the symbol of a new liberty.

Wilfried Ruprecht Bion states that "The incapacity to tolerate empty spaces limits the quantity of spaces available."[7] And a large part of psychoanalytic thinking has followed Bion along these lines, discovering, among the mentally ill, a dimension other than the spatial: an egocentric space attached to a circular notion of time, a space where the void is not negation or absence, but full of living and significant things.

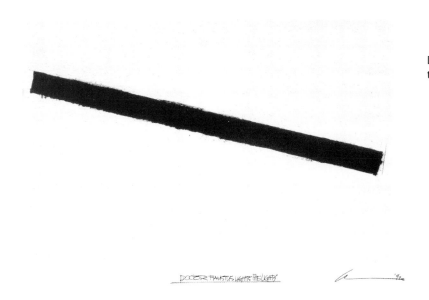

Doctor Faustus Lights
the Lights, 1992. Poster.

As with children's drawings, in the world of the mentally ill, spatial simultaneity is lived as a temporal sequence, where relationships are the basis of meaning.

"The space-time dimension of the mentally ill, of children, and of some groups of people brings to mind the space-time dimension of Albert Einstein. In the theory of relativity there is no absolute space, independent from the observer. The central element in the universe is the space-time unified force. Most oriental philosophies already claimed that space and time are constructions of the mind. For oriental mystics the two basic elements of the mode of formation of the cosmos are the oneness of the universe and its intrinsic dynamism. The non-finite and dynamic present of the Orientals brings to mind Einstein's curved space, as well as the fullness of the void, as it appears in drawings or pictures made by mentally ill people and by children."[8]

The possibility of an opening up of the mind, and the hypothesis that the mind might have total freedom, appears in modern art, in handwriting, in physical and mental behavior patterns, in the sense of color and space, and in studying children and the mentally ill. In these states individuals show, in their attitude towards people and things, an unaffected innocence, free from cultural pressures or social conditioning.

In *Madame Butterfly*, for example, the child is the only one who moves about the stage with pleasure and with freedom, unlike the other characters who follow rigid predetermined movements. The child is also the only character to touch the ground with his hands, and to look up to the sky.

Malevich offers no therapy: "… in the true madhouse, the interns make sure that there are no guns, whereas our government does the opposite and manufactures arms while teaching its crazy followers how to use them efficiently…. In the madhouse, the mad are governed by the sane, while in the outside world the sane are governed by the mad." In Wilson, however, there are only reflections on presumed normality, without any curative intention, in his work with Christopher Knowles, with children, and with people with cerebral palsy. The idea of normality in these cases is closely examined to see how in this "oddity" can be found unexpected stimuli which can broaden consciousness beyond prejudices and conditioning.

Avoidance, insincerity, banality are not part of these worlds. The development of a person who is free can be compared to the artistic process, except that far from dispensing with the need for therapy to make oppres-

the CIVIL warS, act I,
scene C, 1984. Drawing.

sion bearable, this development insists on the elimination of the oppression entirely, replacing it with free and unprejudiced action.

It is not difficult to see the suprematist and non-objective works of Malevich as the clearest precedent to part of the artistic search in America in the 1950s and 1960s. This search made the use of rectangles, the conscious and symbolic use of basic geometric elements its own expressive mark (Robert Morris, Donald Judd). Just as with Malevich's *Black Square*, the works of the minimalists use objects without any internal relationships, objects that do not present problems of "inherent reading."

Wilson's awareness of minimalism must have been acute and innate, starting with an installation like *Poles* in 1967. When young, Wilson was certainly aware of the following works and others like them:

Carl Andre: *I–VIII* of 1966; *8 CUTS* of 1967; *Small Weathering* of 1971 (small squares in various metals, or silicone/chalk bricks which were spread out over the floor of the gallery, in elementary geometric shapes);

Donald Judd: *Untitled, To Dave Shackman* of 1964, made with plumbing pipes; or his cubes in copper, brass, or galvanized iron, from 1966 to 1972. Judd lived and had his studio on Spring Street in Soho, the same street where Wilson moved in 1967 to found and direct the Byrd Hoffman group;

Robert Morris: *Untitled* in his show at the Green Gallery in 1964, (parallelepipeds in varnished compressed wood) or his sculptures in punched steel sheeting;

Bruce Nauman: *Green Light Corridor* of 1970;

Dan Flavin: *The Nominal Tree (To William of Ockam)* of 1963 and *Monument for V. Tatlin* of 1969, a work that paid homage to the poetry of suprematism in its use of fluorescent tubes which dematerialize space.

Other works have influenced Wilson's art–from the Italian branch of *arte povera*, Luciano Fabro's *Vetro di Murano e shantung di seta pura* of 1968-72, in which a large glass bird claw emerges from a leg of cloth hung from the ceiling; and his *Italia* of 1968, where a model of the Italian peninsula is hung, upside down, from the ceiling; or Mario Merz's *Object cache toi* of 1968, using neon and yellow clay to give a crackled effect, reminiscent of the cracks made by Alberto Burri.

D.D.&D. II, act I, scene II, 1987. Drawing.

To see the influence on Wilson, one has only to think of his gigantic cat claw which crosses the stage in *The King of Spain* (1969); or of the colossal elephant foot in *Memory of a Revolution* (1987); or of the trees hung upside down in *G. A. Story* (G. A. for Giorgio Armani, 1996). The notice he paid to Italian radical design with the mention of the armchair *MIES* (1969) by the Archizoom group in *D. D. & D.* should also be noted, as should that paid to Asnago and Vender, Italian forerunners from between the wars, not simply "less is more," but a clear and specific "in less is more."

Wilson's development comes from many complex sources. They range from university studies in economics and finance, to recent work with children's theater groups, and his help to children with cerebral palsy; from going to the Pratt Institute in Brooklyn in 1962, to studying painting in Paris with George McNeil, to the period he spent in the summer of 1966 at Nuova Cosanti working with Paolo Soleri, the Italian architect who since 1956 has been creating a unique architectonic utopia in Paradise Valley, Arizona, with strange philosophical and mystical aspects. The influence of the thought and the architecture of Soleri on Wilson has been more than marginal. This architect, after flirting with minimalism (Dome House, 1949), turned toward forms which are totally alien to all contemporary iconography, preferring composition based on symbolic forms (the circle as an ancient diagram for the reunion of men, the void as the generating element of space) imbued with a vision which is distinctly anti-material. He tried to recover a sense of rite and of archaic myth, taken especially from North American Indians, with a way of working based on very long construction periods and on collaboration. Cosanti was built over a period of eighteen years, from 1956 to 1974, based on a competition for summer work camps there.

191

"THE FOREST" (A WORK IN 7 ACTS)

Although with totally different formal effects, these elements later entered Wilson's theater work. For a whole generation of artists (from music to painting, from writing to staging) it has seemed possible to transform time lived into space lived by using a development of time that shows the author's hope of creating an open relationship between the subjective and objective world, a connection between the visible and the invisible, between the spectator and the work–all within the objective of a rediscovery of the totality of the immaterial, detached from the restrictions of the everyday and of the incidental. "There is no 'inside' to minimalist works. To put it another way, there is no space given for virtual-illusionary meanings to be read into them. What one sees is what they are, made as they are of elementary forms: a cube is a cube, and nothing else; there has been a total drying up of inner meanings. These have been expunged, thrown out." [9]

"American artists of the 1960s tried to reduce the figurative to elemental marks, which they call basic in a space empty of meaning: the sculptors reduced sculpture to a geometric and metaphysical structure, while painters reduced paintings to a mathematical and metaphysical one ... all in a space where emotion springs from the suspense of something which happens in a total void, a logic for which we are unprepared, as happened (a bit imprecisely) in certain works of Edward Hopper." [10]

The meaning of this void–existential, social, and physical–pervades minimalist works, which, precisely because of this absence of things, need endless contact with the public to be accepted. It is not by chance that Sartre and Merleau-Ponty are often mentioned in connection with minimalist work.

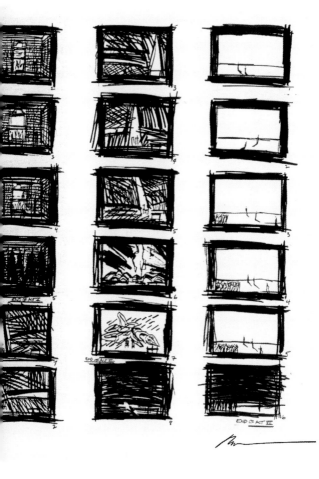

The Forest, 1988. Storyboard.

For minimalism one can in fact put forward a set of principles based on a phenomenological ontology: being is absolute opacity, corresponding to the total inertia of material, which is what it is, and nothing more. "One can only speak about (minimalist) works if that absolute plane is decongested by the void brought to it by the observer; that is, the relationship is made by he who is looking and who decides to move around that meteorite-like thing, fallen from nowhere." [11]

Simplicity, essentiality, radicality—never indulgent nor indulged by the minimalist object—does not, however, mean a simplicity of function. Emptied, as in Malevich's work, of any possibility of interior life, the primitive minimalist object can be seen from a vast and rich series of external viewpoints by the spectator who can make of them whatever he will. An unlimited series of phenomena and of apparitions opens in space and in time. This is not in any way novel if one recalls that Saint Teresa of Avila recommended to the Sisters to trace around their feet on the floor a circle in chalk in order to watch miraculous things happen; or if one thinks of contemplation, like Zen.

Beyond any mysticism, minimalism's results—including its social ones (its opposition to pop art, Wilson's terror of the supermarket)—have helped form new attitudes. These include the rediscovery of a non-violent side of art; the viewer is no longer submerged or drowned in an avalanche of unequivocal messages; the viewer is put on the same level as the work, which, significantly, comes down off the wall to lie down simply, preferably on the floor, in a clear and precise "democratic" reference to equality. The "floorness" of the minimalists is

Orlando, 1989. *Little Door,*
cm 13.3x2x26.

clearly also a homage to the ground, and a rejection of any authoritarian verticality.

Another interesting aspect of minimalism, in conclusion, is the gigantic quality of much of the work of those years—a precaution against any return towards the flame of interiorness, with objects smaller than we are: one might be tempted to turn them again into objects with spiritual meanings. This great size of minimalist things would be used by Wilson to give full and powerful expression to his stagings.

The space-time dimension, action as representative of the void, the possibility of seeing the invisible—these elements were among many others in a fundamental show called, *Portrait, Still Life, Landscape* at the Boymans-van Beuningen Museum in 1993. Facing each other along a corridor, ten little "rooms" were arranged in the form of a parallelepiped. In each of these rooms, like in a *camera ottica*, one or more works from the museum's collection were placed in a stage arrangement of mute dialogues, relationships, subtle emblematic silences. The general effect of non-place was emphasized by the corridor itself, which was almost dematerialized by Dan Flavin's artificial colored and fluorescent lights. These evoked, on a larger scale, the *Green Light Corridor* of Bruce Nauman. In this lost, forsaken place, the visitor was almost sucked into the rooms: the new horizons of vision.

The works of art shown were divested of all inherent meaning, or of meanings placed on them by culture and by history, and then put into an alien place where time had stopped, and thought was suspended. The works became silent presences, without past or future.

This simple radicalness, this apparent reduction, this brave essentiality, suggests that unusual meanings may appear in the works, which could open up a marvelous new life for them. Once they have been "liberated" from that old life, they will spring up with new points of view, phenomena, apparitions.

As he does with his theater work, Wilson brings life to the innate.

At the Boymans Museum, Wilson also set up a little theater: an enormous stage and just a few seats placed very near the stage. Onto the stage, a simple ground with a symbolic horizon-line and a big, wide-open sky, he put a *Ballerina* by Edgar Degas, a *Lucertola* by Hans van Houwelingen of 1992, and a crab, also in bronze, of the sixteenth century. By carefully calculated effects of rising and decreasing light, and of background noise, the scene came alive, making the crab and the lizard seem to move and to threaten the ballerina, and even the spec-

Death Destruction and Detroit,
1979. *Rudolf Hess Beach Chairs*.

Doktor Faustus, 1989.
Esmeralda's Sofa, cm 208x47x92.

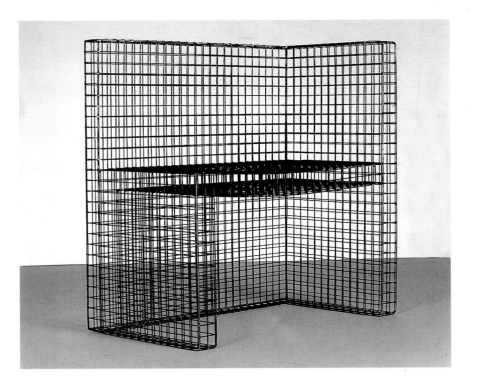

Doktor Faustus, 1989. *Faustus
Mesh Chair*, cm 80x45x75.

Cosmopolitan Greetings,
1988. *Breakfast Chairs.*

tators. It was an example, among many in Wilson's work, in which mental void, rigor, simplicity, the use of basic elements, silence, and the suspension of any thought, open up new ways of seeing, and even of seeing what is not there or what is not happening.

Exemplary of this are the choreography and staging of *Madame Butterfly*. The elements used by Wilson for *Madame Butterfly* are few, basic, and highly effective in making a sort of distillation of language: the floor with a few steps on slightly different levels, the horizon line, the sky-background, and a few objects—an armchair for waiting, a sword (which is sometimes indicated with sword-like gestures), the headrest, the rock. Each object is anti-descriptive, made for an abstract play, calculated mathematically, in which the actors have to submit to an iron alphabet of gestures. All this to avoid any subjectivity—both from famous actors not used to the poetry of Wilson, and for novices chosen for their innocence.

"In Roberto's theater, actors were the stage while the inanimate objects declaimed loudly their anima ... the actors chant mute parliaments while the stage props sing with deep-voiced images." [12]

All the things used by Wilson refine minimalist tradition to the highest degree. The "floorness" is a negation of authoritarian verticalism in favor of the surface of the ground, the "humble base of our existence." [13] Objects are built or made without limiting their form in any way by making them express whatever they are to be used for—such as the armchair for waiting, in black lacquer and bamboo. The chair is totally deprived of anything artistic or pictorial; it is abstract, like a suprematist composition in which the materials used are all different.

On the subject of the importance of the chair in Wilson's theater work and installations (from *Deafman Glance* to *G. A. Story*) it is particularly useful to quote Emilio Ambasz: "When the curtains were drawn on Wilson's mystical landscapes, the state beyond was revealed. A chair on this stage spoke more eloquently of man's form than its intended human user could have. His chairs ... sometimes built with a tilt, or three times larger than normal scale, longingly evoked man's figure. His chair suggested man's imagined majesty more regally than crowned actors. The sometimes roughly-finished wooden surfaces exulted in the unblemished joys of their skin with a gripping strength that no large-screen projection of an actress's face may ever elicit. This chair's lonely

inhabitance of his sidereal landscapes evoked images of pre-linguistic human figures yet to appear, or perhaps,

**Portrait, Still Life,
Landscape**, 1993.
Room II. Boymans-
van Beuningen
Museum, Rotterdam.

Portrait, Still Life, Landscape, 1993. Room III. Boymans-van Beuningen Museum, Rotterdam.

to return. Wilson's chairs spoke of love for the human body with the power of the idealized, as sometimes only love letters to a yet-to-be found lover can elicit. These mystical chairs were solid, trustworthy, and made of a seemingly eternal matter with not an ounce of deceit in them. They could neither disappoint, age, or die as could the human figure they stood for. They were both its surrogate and its alter ego." [14]

The value given to the chair, an object which supports both a person's physical and spiritual weight, is that of a repository of memories and souls, that of powerful metaphors.

Here, Wilson is able once again to make the invisible and the figuratively inexpressible, visible. He manages to set off a whole group of visualizations and memories in time and space, by–note it well–using an object which is particularly static.

That the chair is a symbolic element of great importance in Wilson's world can be seen in the types of chairs used, and by its repeated presence on his stages and in his installations.

In the last decades Wilson's productions have featured the unusable deck-chair in clusters of metal (*Rudolf Hess Beach Chair* in *D. D. & D.*, 1979); the chairs made of plumbing pipes (*Paul Walter Dining Room Suite*, 1980); *Queen Victoria Chairs* (1977), which face each other bulkily with disturbing headlights towards the end; the Shaker-type chairs in wood for *the CIVIL warS* (1985); *Herod's Throne* (1987–90), in which the simplest possible thing to sit on, made of a parallelepiped and a cylinder, is incorporated into an oversized structure; *Society Chair* in *Parzival* (1987), with its legs in the shape of birds' claws; *Chair with a Shadow* (1987), in which the structure of the chair is infused with its double; *Judge's Throne* (*The Martyrdom of St. Sebastian*, 1988) made of heavy geometric blocks halfway between archaic and suprematist; *Esmeralda's Sofa* (*Doktor Faustus*, 1988) in which the chair and the table are one single form as in the work of Donald Judd; *Heinrich Chair* (*Lohengrin*, 1990) with large steps of development contradicted by the occasional lack of support; and *President Chair* (*Canton's Death*, 1992) with its incorporated footrest and carpet.

The chair is a repository for memory as well as a symbol of the static; together these form Wilson's time-span: the negation of movement as something that is only apparent.

In *Deafman Glance*, and then after many years in *G. A. Story*, not only is the chair on stage, but also there are the tortoise and the corridor. This is a clear reference to the paradox of the pre-Socratic philosopher, Zeno of Elea: it would be impossible for Achilles to reach the tortoise, because in the time it took him to cover the ground between them, the tortoise would have moved. Movement, which unquestionably seems to be a sensory impression, has nothing really to do with the essential: the essential is a purely metaphysical thing involving thought – something quite apart from experience. In this, Wilson's manner of making images is similar to that of Giorgio di Chirico, the "master of enigma": the same simple geometric plane, sometimes like a real stage with wooden flooring, as in *Le muse inquietanti* (1918), on which have been placed allegorical statues, people, objects; the same abstract background; the same irreverence towards the obvious and the banal taken so seriously to be

**Portrait, Still Life,
Landscape**, 1993.
Room IV. Boymans-
van Beuningen
Museum, Rotterdam.

Portrait, Still Life, Landscape, 1993.
Large room. Boymans-van Beuningen Museum,
Rotterdam.

objective and real. The same lack of logic in the compositional elements: the little train which, like Wilson's corridor, heads toward the line of the horizon.

The quality of symbolic rite in Wilson's theater-pieces, his meticulous dedication and attention to every detail of the scenes (objects and actors are considered as joint elements), the central importance of the void and of silence, the solemnity which pervades the action, the anti-natural and anti-psychological feelings of the movements, the sounds, the use of repetition–these are all symbolic elements. They are the words, the colors capable of carrying the imagination of the observer towards the invisible: a cosmic invisibility to which man belongs and to which anyone must refer in order to give true value to actions and thoughts.

It was in the 1970s that Wilson's theater was most widely produced and acclaimed. Two of his more illustrious colleagues have commented simply and fundamentally on his apparent distance from even the most prosaic reality, and upon the social and political commitment of his work. On the one hand, Heiner Müller: "When we met for the first time, Wilson asked me what my earliest childhood memory was: for him the first memory was of a supermarket, an image of terror. For me it was looking through a keyhole to see three Nazis taking my father away. So we agreed that there are two types of terror, political and commercial." [15] On the other hand, Pina Bausch, when asked about her favorite type of theater, told of two people talking about *Einstein on the Beach*. "The first: to me the best moment was when the white horse walked across the stage. The second: But there wasn't any white horse! The first: But I saw it clearly!!" Pina Bausch concludes, "Any theater where such a thing is possible, this I find beautiful." [16]

Wilson's criticism is certainly directed towards utilitarian consumer society and towards its absolute lack of ideals, but this is a criticism in symbols–obscure, indirect.

Theater becomes the means to make visible symbols of the unknown, through form, color, sound, and action. These are used normally and without arbitrary external forms. Everyday anxiety, which certainly exists, becomes the symbol of a human state, fighting its battles within a modern mythology, with monsters, chasms, vertigo–in a sort of explosive mix of Joyce's *Ulysses*, and the absurd laws of a Kafka-esque court house.

This discomfort is more existential in nature than directly social. The attempts, therefore, of certain critics to see precise implications (in the context of the Reagan and Bush years) in the various performances of *Einstein on the Beach*, which is a homage to the light, the pure science, and the humanity of Einstein, are not really productive.

Acting symbolically, Wilson's goal is to have an effect on basic things, avoiding repetition of whatever is already there (this is where his anti-naturalism comes from, his escape from whatever is limiting, and from the press). Instead, he stimulates an acute consciousness of the real by enlarging the mind and its intuitive sixth sense to search for an authentic art. In a sort of poetic modern rendering of the sublime, we watch the rebirth of wonder, of weightlessness, of ecstatic contemplation, of silence before a mysterious rediscovered sense of truth, of the dignity of man, and of his insistent questions to find sense in life.

Like a modern alchemist, Wilson has investigated an enormous complex of artistic experiences in this century (from the metaphysical to surrealism, from minimalism to *arte povera*, from abstraction to clear expressionism) using an experimental method aimed at perfection, at distillation, at transformation into a something precious.

Robert Wilson's original way of speaking, his persistent interior monologue which culminated in 1995 with *HAMLET: a Monologue*, the innocence of his vision, so simply and candidly able to re-see and re-discover anything, his silent and disturbing characters, his bare stages which force one to struggle inside, but which regenerate and change–all this; his insistent search for another meaning to life–will continue to reverberate for a long time.

Notes

[1] F. Pivano, "Il Minimalismo di Raymond Carver," in R. Carver, *Di cosa parliamo quando parliamo d'amore*, Milan, 1987.

[2] F. Carmagnola, V. Pasca, "Minimalism and Design in the Nineties," *Lotus* 81, 1994.

[3] M. Eliade, *Immagini e simboli. Saggi sul simbolismo magico religioso*, Milan, 1981.

[4] W. Kandinsky, *Tutti gli scritti*, Milan, 1973.

[5] W. Worringer, *Astrazione e empatia*, Turin, 1975.

[6] K. Malevic, *Suprematismo*, Bari, 1969.

[7] W. R. Bion, *Lemen durch Erfahrungen*, Frankfurt, 1990.

[8] E. Venturini, *Lo spazio di confine, costellazione di eventi e di possibilità*, Imola, 1995.

[9] R. Barilli, "Minimalismo, Land Art, Art-Form," in *L'Arte Moderna*, Milan, 1977.

[10] F. Pivano, op. cit.

[11] R. Barilli, op. cit.

[12] E. Ambasz, "Working Fables: A Collection of Design for Skeptic Children," in *Architecture and Urbanism* 5, May 1980.

[13] R. Barilli, op. cit.

[14] E. Ambasz, op. cit.

[15] H. Müller, "Il Patalogo," 1988.

[16] P. Bausch, "Die Zeit," 9.2.1979.

Robert Stearns

BEFORE THE DEAFMAN GLANCED

Listen to the pictures

Robert Wilson[1]

If among you are
those who wish to get
somewhere
let them leave at
any moment

John Cage [2]

The appearance of *Deafman Glance* on the stage of the University Theater in Iowa City in 1970 signaled a major transition in Bob Wilson's life and work. It was performed again in 1971 at the Brooklyn Academy and toured in Europe, appearing in France in Nancy and Paris, as well as in Rome and in Amsterdam. That exposure brought Wilson's work to the attention of critics, artists and audiences throughout Europe, and it was the beginning of a life-long relationship between Wilson and the theater and opera centers of France, Italy, Holland, and Germany.

Like most watershed events in the lives of creative artists, though, it didn't emerge from thin air. It was a plateau in the then thirty-year-old Wilson's career that opened doors and gave him the opportunity to expand and evolve his already complex talents. He has come to be considered by many to be "among the greatest theater-makers of the twentieth century."[3] While that is true, it doesn't adequately encompass Wilson's broad reach as an artist. He is not so much a theater-maker as a rigorous tutor who uses the stage (among many arenas) to focus *our* attention on the world around us, on the things in it, and ultimately on the beauty and mystery of human endeavor.

My goal here is to outline some of the facets of Wilson's undertakings that spill out of the boundaries of the theater, and to offer a glimpse of the forces in his life that have contributed to his remarkable achievements. To do that, it is best to begin at the beginning. Several writers and biographers have sketched Bob's formative years, but none have put it down as completely yet succinctly as Laurence Shyer:

1941–1962

Robert Mims Wilson is born in Waco, Texas, on October 4, 1941. First child of Loree (Hamilton) and D. M. Wilson, attorney and later city manager of Waco.

As a child of eight or nine, he presents plays in his garage with his grandmother and the girl next door. At the age of seventeen he is cured of a stammer with the help of Miss Byrd ("Baby") Hoffman, a local dance instructor, who teaches him to speak slowly and free the tension from his body through movement. During his junior high and high school years, Wilson appears in school plays and in productions presented by the Waco Children's Theater (Jearnine Wagner, director) and Baylor University Teenage Theatre, and participates in speech contests and debates. He graduates from Waco High School in the spring of 1959.

Enters the University of Texas (Austin) the following fall, majoring in business administration. He begins working with brain-damaged children and children's theater groups. In the spring of 1962, a year before his scheduled graduation, he drops out to pursue a career in design and the arts. [4]

This brief outline covers a lot of territory with a minimum of fliss. In it we learn that Wilson was raised in an established, middle-class family in a medium-sized, mid-Texas town. We meet his grandmother, who joined him in some performances later on. We meet Jearnine Wagner, who invited him back to Texas after he moved to New York, and we meet Miss Byrd Hoffman, whose dance instructions had probably the most significant impact on the formation of Wilson's view of himself and the world. We learn that he was aware of the relationship between physical and mental well-being and that he shared the understanding he gained from Byrd Hoffman with others, particularly those who lived with disabilities on the margins of society. We learn that, in an effort to please his parents, he gained an education in business administration. And, we learn that he rejected that career, choosing instead to pursue a more sympathetic direction in the arts.

Moving to New York in the fall of 1962, Bob enrolled at Pratt Institute in Brooklyn to study architecture and interior design. He followed a loosely structured course of education in design, architecture, and painting and applied what he was learning to the creation of a number of multi-media events that combined dance, music, and art. During this time he discovered the choreography of Martha Graham, Merce Cunningham, and Alwin Nikolais. After seeing one of Martha Graham's performances he wrote to her to express his delight and excitement with her work, and was rewarded with an invitation to observe classes at her studio. Bob was quiet and somewhat reserved, but he has never shy about introducing himself to people who interested him. He did the same with Alwin Nikolais who, after a conversation backstage following a performance, invited Wilson to work with him and his collaborator, Murray Louis. Bob created sets and costumes for some of their music/dance events and was greatly influenced by their experiments in integrating dance with theater and music and visual design. In 1963, he experimented with film, creating a brief, ten-minute abstract work titled *Slant* for WNET-TV.

In the summer of 1964, he traveled to Europe for the first time and studied painting with George McNeil, the American abstract expressionist who was on the Pratt faculty and was in residence at the American Center in Paris. Returning to New York in the fall of 1964, Wilson designed sets for *Landscapes* and *Junk Dances* by Murray Louis, and created several of his own works that combined movement, lighting, costumes, and film to the accompaniment of music and noise. Among them were a dance with film performed during his junior year at Pratt at the New York State Pavilion at the New York World's Fair, and *Duricglte & Tomorrow,* a dance/theater event that featured foil-covered poles, floating mobiles, colored lights, and the Baroque music of Praetorius competing for attention with the sound of banging hammers. In the spring of 1965, Wilson designed sets and costumes for the Café La Mama production of *America Hurrah!* by Jean Claude van Itallie.

Throughout this time, Wilson continued the work he had begun in Texas with brain-damaged and disturbed children. Unlike many artists who had left small towns in search of creative freedom that could be pursued in larger cities, Wilson did not abandon contact with friends and family at home. In the summer of 1965, at the invitation of his former teacher, Jearnine Wagner, he conducted classes in painting and movement at Trinity University in San Antonio. Two works came from these classes, one of which he substituted for a more conventional play he had intended to present. As Laurence Shyer describes, "[It] featured some of the visual elements and actions he would use in his later works. Three actors in a white room (Wilson among them) were seen performing simple tasks in silence: walking, sitting, putting on a glove, tracing a line across the floor with sand, leaning against a wire."[5] The second, performed in Waco, was a work titled *Modern Dance,* a melange of events that spoofed the Miss America contest with detergent cartons as props, a sound track medley of patriotic songs, gospel hymns, and the Miss America theme song. Commenting in Wilson's home-town newspaper, the *Waco Tribune Herald,* in July, 1965, Gynter Quill wrote, "It is too early yet to even guess what will become of Robert Wilson, particularly since he himself isn't sure. He may be an architect who paints or produces experimental films, or he may be a producer who turns to interior architecture when he wants to eat."[6]

Back in New York after his summer in Texas, Wilson continued taking classes at Pratt, created two dances *(Clorox* and *Opus 2)* which were presented in the spring of 1966, and, at the invitation of Jerome Robbins, observed and taught classes at the American Theater Laboratory before graduating in June. He took another summer away from New York to work on the construction of the utopian community of Arcosanti, near Scottsdale, Arizona, which was being created by the visionary architect Paolo Soleri. He attempted to continue painting but found it increasingly difficult and unsatisfying and finally suffered a nervous breakdown. He attempted suicide and was committed to a mental institution for several months.

After his recovery, he returned to New York in 1967 and rented a loft studio at 147 Spring Street in the neighborhood south of Houston Street that was yet to be dubbed SoHo. The loft had previously been occupied by the Open Theater, the seminal experimental theater company directed by Joseph Chaikin. The Spring Street studio

The King of Spain,
New York, 1969.

would soon become the home of one of the era's most unique creative collectives, made up of people who gathered around Wilson as he conceived new works, assembled performance workshops, taught classes in New York and New Jersey, and as he earned a living as a special instructor for the Department of Welfare and the New York Board of Education. For Wilson, there was little demarcation between his approach to dance and theater and to his work with his mentally and physically challenged clients. The resolution of his own speech problems through the guidance of Byrd Hoffman provided the methods that he applied to performance and to therapy. Explaining later, he recalled that she "talked to me about the energy in my body, about relaxing, letting energy flow through. … She would play piano and I would move my body. She didn't watch…. She never taught a technique, she never gave me a way to approach it, it was more that I discovered it on my own."[7]

This reliance on self-discovery, non-judgmental reinforcement of each person's interests and abilities, and above all, mental and physical discipline, is the core of Wilson's process and the source of his charisma, which attracted a motley but fascinating coterie to the Spring Street loft. The group came to be comprised of "drop-ins" escaping middle-class boredom, co-workers from various hospitals, other artists, and students from his art and dance workshops. In honor of Byrd Hoffman, Wilson for a while took her name and called the group and the loft the Byrd Hoffman School of Byrds. The Byrd Hoffman Foundation was formed in 1969 to produce and tour the events they created. With the "Byrds," as they came to be known, Wilson created many of his first large works, including *The King of Spain, The Life and Times of Sigmund Freud, Deafman Glance, KA MOUNTAIN AND GUARDenia TERRACE, The Life and Times of Joseph Stalin, A Letter for Queen Victoria, The $ Value of Man,* and finally *Einstein on the Beach.* It is beyond the scope of this writing to recount the stories of this singular group of people. Some participated in only a few productions, others have remained close friends and associates.

During the early Byrd Hoffman years, in 1967 and 1968, he constructed dance and theater events that explored sound and word repetition, attenuated movement, silence, and a-logical juxtaposition. He culled material from any and every resource at hand: advertisements, pop songs, and fragments of ideas he appreciated in other artists' works. Not infrequently, some of his fellow artists were surprised and chagrined to recognize in Wilson's work some prop or gesture or movement notion that they had used recently in their own work. It would be

inaccurate not to point this out, not just to atone for minor crimes of plagiarism, but to address a central issue that was already developing in his work: his method of appropriating and assembling material into what would soon become large and complex works. Collage, assemblage and montage were techniques that painters, sculptors, and filmmakers had been exploring for several decades. Picasso, Braque, Schwitters, Duchamp, Dali, Magritte, (Merrit) Oppenheim, Cocteau, Cornell, and so many others, had been gathering unrelated images and objects and recomposing them for years. Wilson was beginning to apply this idea to theater. Later, in the 1980s, critics and aestheticians in the visual arts would dub such borrowing "appropriation" and herald it as a hallmark of post-modernism.

Adopting the alter-ego of Byrd Hoffman, or the Byrdwoman, Wilson created *BYRD woMAN* in the fall of 1968. The event began at the Spring Street loft with Wilson dressed in his Byrdwoman costume. He and the Byrds, plus the noted choreographer and composer Meredith Monk, performed simple movements such as bouncing on boards and leaning on stretched wires. The audience was then transported on flatbed trucks to Jones Alley, where many of the visual elements were repeated, and Wilson appeared again as the Byrdwoman while forty similarly dressed figures appeared on nearby rooftops and fire escapes.

These modestly scaled events led to the 1969 production of *The King of Spain,* his largest and most ambitious work up to that time, presented on the proscenium stage of the deteriorating Anderson Theater on Second Avenue in New York City. As vanguard as his works had appeared to be up to this point, *The King of Spain* was a foray into the illusionistic space of traditional theater, and it demonstrated Bob's mysterious ability to combine convention with experiment, to join formal discipline with aleatoric dissonance. The performance included three scenes: a beach, a Victorian drawing room, and a cave. Trevor Fairbrother describes one of the sets:

> [The] *trompe l'oeil* backdrops … painted by Fred Koluch (now Kolo) depicted a musty Victorian drawing room. A central high-back chair was turned away from the audience to face a doorway; in it sat an indistinct red-haired figure, presumed to be the King. To the left a floor-to-ceiling strip cut from the wall revealed a sunny landscape with distant mountains and sea. Entering through the door, a great variety of people slowly assembled. Eventually they filed out behind the thirty-foot-high legs of what was imagined to be a gigantic cat crossing the stage. At the last moment the King broke his motionless vigil,

standing and turning; the audience saw his hairy paws (reminiscent of those in Cocteau's film *Beauty and the Beast)* and a grotesque mask face.[8]

Fairbrother continues with the following excerpt from a review of the performance written by Stephen Smoliar:

> Ranging in age from seven to seventy, [the cast] spent an hour being interesting by being themselves. Completely unaware of the presence of an audience, three men involved themselves moving geometrical objects about a chess board, one woman decorated herself with black feathers, and another woman talked incessantly about all sorts of nothing. ... It might go well in a museum room, where one could walk in, stand around for a while, go look at something else, and come back later to see if anything new was happening."[9]

With *The King of Spain,* Wilson began to focus on the composition of rich and complex stage pictures, spaces in which time and light were used to frame casual and apparently unrelated activities; a collage of objects, people, textures, shapes, and lines. Later that year, Harvey Lichtenstein, then newly appointed director of the Brooklyn Academy of Music and himself a former student of Martha Graham, invited Wilson to create a work for BAM. Bob reassembled parts of *The King of Spain* and added many more images to create the four-hour *The Life and Times of Sigmund Freud,* which he called a "hybrid dance play." John Perrault wrote in the *Village Voice,* "I no longer know the difference between theater and dance and art.... [This is] a beautiful artwork, no matter what the category. [It] had so little obvious meaning that it contained all meanings.... It was static yet full of activities. The arrangement of the incidents was musical rather than literary.... It was one of the strangest things I have ever seen in my life."[10]

The next step was *Deafman Glance,* first staged at the University Theater at the University of Iowa in late 1970, at the time one of the most fertile oases of creative energy in the country. It was staged again in 1971 at the Brooklyn Academy of Music and became Europe's introduction to Robert Wilson when it toured four cities there.

Notes

1 L. Shyer, *Robert Wilson and his Collaborators*, New York, 1989, xv.

2 Musée national d'art moderne, *MR BOJANGLE'S MEMORY og son of fire*, n.p.

3 Shyer, op. cit., back cover.

4 Shyer, op. cit., 288.

5 Shyer, op. cit., 293.

6 G. Quill, *Waco Herald Tribune*, July 25, 1965.

7 S. Brecht, *The Theatre of Visions: Robert Wilson*, Frankfurt, 1978, 14.

8 T. Fairbrother, *Robert Wilson's Vision*, Boston, 1991, 112.

9 Ibid.

10 J. Perrault, "Art: Trying Harder," *Village Voice*, Jan. 1, 1970, 16.

Robert Stearns

TANGIBLE LOGIC: WILSON'S VISUAL ARTS

Robert Wilson moves freely between the temporal media of theater, film, and sound and the spatial media of drawing, sculpture, and architecture. Wilson's work is consistent with, even emblematic of the syncretic tendencies of twentieth-century aesthetics. Trained as a visual artist, Bob gives an unusual measure of attention to the physical attributes of his stage arena: both the composition of the overall tableaux and their details. Conversely, he gives attention to the temporal attributes of his physical objects and designs. Some of Wilson's works are ephemeral, some are durable. The durable variety includes drawings, sculpture, installations, exhibition designs, interiors, and most recently, free-standing buildings.

Some observers have pointed to the contradiction between the formal look of his work and the apparent chaos of unrelated images and actions. And that is indeed the beauty and utter appropriateness of his art in these times. Beneath the anarchy of discordant voices, unrelated movements and actions lies a clear structure, a disciplined and simple order that ties everything together. We can grasp this order most clearly through Wilson's physical objects because their architectural logic lies so close to the surface.

Drawings

Drawing is a fundamental thinking process for Wilson, as it is for many artists. From quick cocktail-napkin and back-of-envelope sketches to more studied efforts, Bob's drawings are notes and outlines for his scenography. Ever since 1969, when *The King of Spain* was performed on a proscenium stage, drawings of the stage pictures Bob imagines have been an essential mode of communicating to others what he has in mind. More than a tool of communication, the act of drawing is a step in the formation of the ideas themselves.

Many of Wilson's early drawings incorporated words, the things that unsettled him the most before he met Byrd Hoffman. The word drawings have served as text and also as visual material in some of the performances, particularly in *A Letter for Queen Victoria*, which was created with substantial input from Wilson's protégé, Christopher Knowles. Each word was slowly and deliberately placed on the page, each letter consciously drawn and redrawn: real words like THERE, NOW, and OK; and nonsense syllables like PIRUP, HATH, and SPUPS.

A more conventional playwright begins with a written script. Wilson begins with drawings and diagrams. He might sketch a rectangle and divide it into three parts horizontally, then vertically, creating a chart that serves

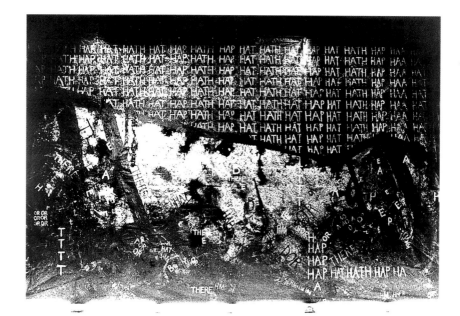

A Letter for Queen Victoria,
1974. Dam Drop.

Einstein on the Beach, 1976. Storyboard.

Einstein on the Beach, 1976. Drawing for Train 1.

I Was Sitting On My Patio…, 1977. Drawing.

Parzival, 1987. Drawing.

Die Materie (Part II), 1989. Drawing.

as an outline of the scenes and acts. The drawing may also become the basis for the design of the stage itself. Wilson explains that he sees space as horizontal and time as vertical. We see this pure formalism transform into a theatrical event when, for example in *Einstein on the Beach*, a horizontal bar of light very slowly rises to a vertical position and ascends into the theater loft. If we have the necessary clues, this manipulation of rigid geometry can become a nearly spiritual experience. The result is a theater of images, a theater of visions.

Virtually all the drawings are black-and-white, created with charcoal or graphite. They are gestural and expressive, and reflect his study of painting. Some drawings depict sequential views of the stage, like a storyboard, showing how the major elements of the stage design evolve from one scene to the next. The remaining drawings, the largest number, are single images showing one moment in the progress of the play.

Wilson's style of drawing has evolved from relatively controlled delineations to increasingly energetic expressions to near-total abstractions. Drawings for *Einstein on the Beach* in 1976 were somewhat naturalistic. The train in a drawing for Act I, for example, is clearly a train with a headlight and smoke curling from its stack. A 1977 drawing of the library scene in *Patio* shows neatly shelved books behind the crisp white lines of the Patio Sofa on the left and a table on the right. By 1983 and 1984, Wilson's hand became looser, more lyrical and assured. The drawings became more dynamic and filled with energy. Still later, as in those for *Parsifal, Doktor Faustus,* and *De Materie,* they were brimming with atmosphere, abstract tempests of light and dark.

The Life and Times of Sigmund Freud, 1969.
Hanging Chair.

Overture, 1972.
Overture Chair.

Einstein on the Beach, 1972.
Einstein Chair.

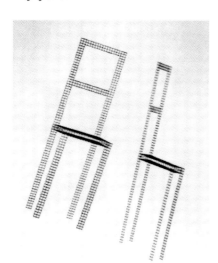

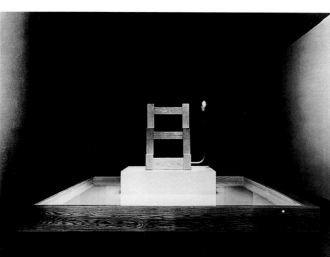

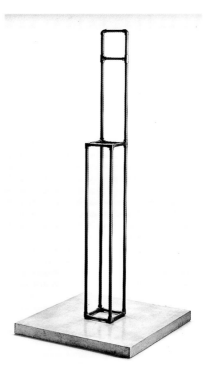

Sculpture

Objects created for use on stage form another important part of Wilson's artistic output. Stage props are a part of most every theatrical production, but Wilson often gives his objects more than utilitarian or decorative functions. They are designed and crafted to be permanent. Since Wilson's works are not naturalistic, their sets are not intended to look like a living room or a tavern or a street corner. Wilson's objects are sometimes imbued with as much presence as the live actors, so he considers their form with appropriate care. Instead of lessening the importance of the actors, Wilson's focus on the shape, proportions, material and color of *every* object on his stage heightens our attention to *all* the details, including the actors.

Chairs are the most frequent form of his sculptures. They are a consistent leitmotif in his productions. The first was *Hanging Chair (Freud Chair)* (1969). Its simple geometry–four straight legs, a flat seat, and a straight back–became the prototypical chair from which Wilson has created variations ever since. Chairs (and stools, benches, sofas, recliners, and by extension, beds) are unique among all utilitarian objects. They exist only to support the weight of people. Since people, and their accumulated deeds and actions in history, are Wilson's underlying and consistent theme, his chairs become potent metaphors, repositories of souls, spiritual reliquaries, holders of memories. The weighty *Overture Chair* (1972) curiously appears to float on water. The *Queen Victoria Chairs* (1974) are weighty, squat, lead-covered thrones burdened with history, while the *Einstein Chair* (1976) is a tall, lean, simple construction of plumbing pipe providing, perhaps, a good vantage point from which to see the future. The highly polished aluminum-slatted *Beach Chairs* (1977) from *Death, Destruction & Detroit (DD&D)* discharge a cold, teutonic self-indulgence. Bob would permit us to indulge in such free associations with later works like *Chair with a Shadow (Parzival,* 1987), *Chair for Marie Curie (De Materie,* 1989), the *Esmeralda Sofa (Doktor Faustus,* 1989), and many more.

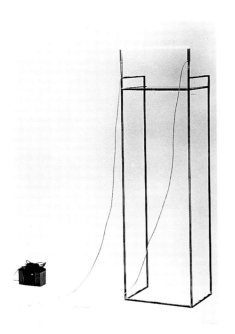

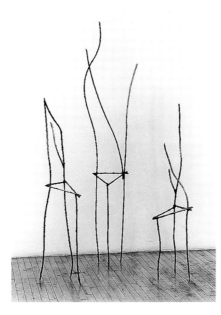

Die Materie, 1989. *Chair for Marie Curie.*

The Magic Flute, 1991. *Amadeus.*

Orlando, 1989. *A bed for Virgina Woolf.*

Installations and Exhibitions

Exhibitions of Wilson's works, other than drawing shows, take a step beyond the conventional displays of dissociated objects. They are arrangements of the space, light, and sound that surround each object. Wilson devises the path the visitor will follow, turning the exhibition into a subtle participatory performance. Along with the sculptures that come from the stage productions, Wilson has created a number of indoor and outdoor installations. The earliest, *Poles,* was created in 1968 during a summer residency at Grailville, a Catholic retreat near Loveland, a small town in southwestern Ohio. The eight-meter-square structure was located, and still stands, in an open field about a quarter mile from Grailville's main buildings. Six hundred and fifty-six used telephone poles were set in rows that rise in equal increments from a height of 75 to 560 centimeters. A trio of square arches forms a ceremonial entrance to the field. Laurence Shyer describes the making of *Poles* in *Robert Wilson and his Collaborators:*

> With his friends Duncan Curtis and Kikuo Saito and members of the Grail community, Wilson spent two-and-a-half months erecting the massive sculpture (as well as an arched entryway of telephone poles) in a wheat field. During construction Wilson danced every night in the nearby chapel. It was there that he conceived the character of the Byrdwoman, a strange figure in a floppy hat and long braids, who was to appear in later works. In the middle of August, Wilson presented a new piece (possibly titled Byrdwoman) with Grail members in the chapel. Another event was staged to celebrate the completion of the project. Upon entering the performance site, spectators found Wilson, dressed as the Byrdwoman, silhouetted against the setting sun. They then helped lay a bed of gray slag around the base of the monument and Wilson threaded a red rubber hose through the poles. [1]

The construction of *Poles* was an event, a group activity: a performance. It is an object but it is also a site for play. Its scale is monumental and human at the same time. Thirty years later, the field surrounding it is still care-

Poles, 1968. Grailville, Loveland, Ohio.

fully mowed, but the narrow spaces between the poles are overgrown with volunteer trees and shrubs, many now taller than the poles themselves. Leafing out in summer and standing bare in winter, the volunteers have created their own organic form that counterpoints the sculpture's austere geometry.

In 1972, as part of series of events that preceded the seven-day performance of *KA MOUNTAIN AND GUARDenia TERRACE* in Iran, Wilson and other members of the School of Byrds held an exhibition at the Musée Galliera in Paris, sponsored by the Festival d'Automne and the Théâtre des Nations. Two years later, the museum assembled a solo exhibition, *Robert Wilson: Dessins et Sculptures,* which included a copper-edged water tank, a stuffed alligator, the hanging chair from *Freud,* the flying bench from *Deafman Glance,* small versions of the *Overture Chair* and *Stalin Chair,* the large *Stalin Chairs,* the *Queen Victoria* chairs, and the large *Overture Chair,* floating in a pool of water outdoors in the museum garden.

Spaceman, created in early 1976 in collaboration with the artist Ralph Hilton, is difficult to categorize as either an installation or a performance. It was Wilson's first use of video and included live performers, yet it was contained within a box-like structure, viewed from all sides like a sculpture. A 365-by-106-by-1980-centimeter construction of wood and translucent plastic film slightly obscured the things and people inside. *Spaceman* was assembled at the time Wilson and Philip Glass were developing *Einstein on the Beach,* and it allowed Wilson to explore several visual elements and themes that he was working on in *Einstein.* A man sat stiffly in a chair with his right hand raised as though writing on a blackboard. A woman sat fishing under a high table. Another man lay suspended on a board overhead, flying like Superman. A grid-wall of video monitors showed an old woman pulling back on a throttle, appearing to fly a jet or a rocket ship. The length of the structure was divided into three sections labeled "portrait," "still life," and "landscape," a trilogy of forms he would call on again in 1993 in an exhibition in Rotterdam. *Spaceman* was recreated in the fall of 1984 for *The Luminous Image,* a group video exhibition organized by the Stedelijk Museum in Amsterdam. This second version included only one live performer.

Several small but important exhibitions were held between 1976 and 1980 at the Iolas Gallery, Marian Goodman Gallery, and Paula Cooper Gallery in New York, and at Galerie Folker Skulima in Berlin and Galerie

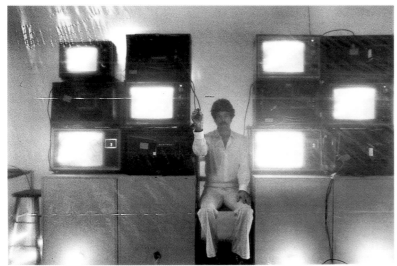

Robert Wilson: Dessins et Sculptures, 1974. Installation view. Musée Galliera, Paris.

Spaceman, 1976. The Kitchen Center for Video and Music, New York.

Robert Wilson: **From a Theater of Images**, 1980. Installation for *I Was Sitting On My Patio*.... The Contemporary Arts Center, Cincinnati.

Robert Wilson: **From a Theater of Images**, 1980. *Queen Victoria Chairs* for *A Letter for Queen Victoria*. The Contemporary Arts Center, Cincinnati.

Robert Wilson: **From a Theater of Images**, 1980. Installation view. Foreground: *Stalin Chairs*. The Contemporary Arts Center, Cincinnati.

Memory of a Revolution,
1987. Installation view.
Staatsgalerie, Stuttgart.

Zwirner in Cologne. These exhibitions, presenting drawings as well as the sculptures that were starting to accumulate from the performances, began to establish Wilson's reputation as a visual artist.

Wilson's second museum exhibition was organized by this author at the Contemporary Arts Center in Cincinnati, Ohio, in 1980, and traveled to the Neuberger Museum in Purchase, New York. *Robert Wilson: From a Theater of Images* assembled most of the sculptures that Wilson had created to date: several large theater backdrops; a selection of drawings from *Queen Victoria, Einstein, Patio* and *DD&D;* a re-creation of a full stage set and lighting from *Patio;* the recently completed version of *Video-50;* and several other works. In his review of the exhibition, Craig Owens observes that it was

> a series of profoundly arresting tableaux that engaged the viewer directly, without reference to their theatrical origins. … The spectator became a participant in a kind of ritual procession to a consecrated site. The effectiveness of [these] images within the museum context was largely the result of Wilson's determination to use its galleries as more than neutral containers for isolated objects. … [He] worked to transform the museum into a theater of encounters. A major factor in this transformation—and in all of Wilson's work—was light. [2]

The exhibition and its accompanying catalog helped to place Wilson's work in the context of the visual arts. They began to address the debate that has still not been resolved as to whether Wilson's visual output is "real" art or just residue from performances.

From 1981 through 1987, most of Wilson's solo exhibitions focused exclusively on drawings produced for stage productions during that time: *the CIVIL warS, The Golden Windows, Parsifal, Medea, Alceste, Alcestis, Hamletmaschine,* and others. A notable exception was a collection of sculptures, drawings, and costumes assembled by the Gallery of Art at the Rhode Island School of Design in early 1983 that also included sculpture and new objects being created for *the CIVIL warS.* In 1987, for the first time, Wilson created a work specifically and only for presentation in a museum. *Memory of a Revolution* was commissioned by the Galerie der Stadt, Stuttgart, in

Robert Wilson's Vision, 1991. Entrance to the exhibition. Museum of Fine Arts, Boston.

commemoration of the French Revolution. It was presented concurrently with an historical exhibition, *Baden-Württemberg in the Age of Napoleon,* and around the time of Stuttgart performances of Wilson's productions *of Alcestis, Alceste,* and *Quartett. Memory of a Revolution* was contained in a room divided into two spaces by a jail-like metal grill. On the side accessible to the viewer was a row of red-upholstered, gilt sidechairs. On the other was a colossal elephant foot with a niche carved into it, in which sat an elderly Napoleon holding the model of a theater set for *Medea.* On a dirt floor, a hundred rubber rats crawled toward the seated figure. The elephant foot recalled the giant cat feet that paraded across the stage in *The King of Spain* in 1969, but it referred specifically to a monumental elephant fountain built by Napoleon, which stood in the Place de la Bastille in the early nineteenth century, and where the new Paris opera house was under construction in 1987. *Memory of a Revolution* was a complex layer of allegories alluding to lofty visions and failed deeds, imprisonment and freedom, history and the future. In this installation, Wilson addressed space, time, and memory for the first time in purely visual, sculptural terms.

A second major retrospective, *Robert Wilson's Vision,* was mounted in 1991 by the Museum of Fine Arts, Boston, curated by Trevor Fairbrother. The exhibition included drawings, sculpture, backdrops, a re-creation of the spaceship scene from *Einstein on the Beach,* and *Memory of a Revolution.* The entire exhibition was infused with a sound environment composed by Wilson's long-time collaborator, Hans Peter Kuhn. For the exhibition, Wilson designed the most structured plan to date, one that reinforced the drama of the viewer's procession. Describing the plan, Fairbrother wrote

Wilson conceived of an exhibition that would unfold like a journey and suggest the passage of a day. His title for the work as a whole was *The Night before the Day.* Passing a television documentary about Wilson, the viewer would enter through a narrow corridor. The first room, spacious and bright, would feature objects (several of them suspended from the ceiling) suggestive of the fanciful flight of the youthful imagination. The middle room, gray, formal, and pivotal, would be densely hung with drawings of all sizes, and would house a smaller room in its center enclosing the bizarre installation piece, *Memory of a*

223

Robert Wilson's Vision, 1991.
Room one. Museum of Fine Arts,
Boston.

Robert Wilson's Vision, 1991. Room three.
Museum of Fine Arts, Boston.

Constructing the model for **MR. BOJANGLE'S MEMORY og son of fire**, 1991.
Centre Georges Pompidou, Paris.

MR. BOJANGLE'S MEMORY og son of fire, 1991. Installation view.
Centre Georges Pompidou, Paris.

Binnenalster Door, m 12x7x1,1992-93.
Installation view. Banks of the Alster River,
Hamburg.

Revolution. The third and last room, open like the first, would foster a contrasting mood with dark walls and an ominous ensemble of objects. [3]

Robert Wilson's Vision revealed the artist's accelerating architectural sophistication, which he applied again in the creation of *MR BOJANGLE'S MEMORY og son of fire,* an exhibition at the Centre Georges Pompidou in Paris in late 1991. The museum invited Wilson to create an exhibition that would be "a journey in which the visitor will be immersed, and which will call upon all the resources of his art, objects and furniture elements borrowed from his performances, along with prized works from the collection of the National Museum of Modern Art, as well as an audiotape that will accompany the visitors on their journey and a videotape specially created for the occasion." [4] The result was an extravagant stroll garden in a post-volcanic disaster zone. What appeared to be a lava flow partially buried a section of highway, and through this field the spectator followed a raised, boardwalk path. Along the path, one encountered chairs from *Freud, Stalin, Queen Victoria, Patio, D.D.&D., Parzival, Faustus,* and more, interspersed among paintings and sculptures from the museums' collection by Brancusi, de Kooning, Andre, Modigliani, Giacometti, Niki de St. Phalle, Yves Klein, and others. The space was animated with video collages and with a sonic environment, again created by Hans Peter Kuhn. Each work was lit with the precision for which Wilson has come to be known on the stage. About the project, Wilson commented, "What pleases me, finally, is that [the museum] is a center for creation, a living place, not a place where one finds dead things" [5] In this exhibition Wilson breathed a new and different kind of life into works of art. Set among his sculptures-as-metaphors-of-life, the works of the other artists became allegories of their creators instead of mute remains of their lives. The sculptures and paintings became actors on Wilson's stage. Here Brancusi, Giacometti, and Yves Klein joined hands with Sigmund Freud, Queen Victoria, Rudolf Hess, and Abraham Lincoln.

The *Binnenalster Door,* constructed in late 1992 and installed in early 1993 in a wide portion of the Alster River in Hamburg, was the first monumental outdoor sculpture Wilson had undertaken since the construction of

Portrait, Still Life, Landscape,
1993. Installation view. Boymans-van
Beuningen Museum, Rotterdam.

Poles in Ohio in 1968. Its form was derived from the small door created for *Orlando,* and is reminiscent of the portal-like shapes that stand several meters from the main portion of the *Poles* sculpture. Hovering mysteriously in the water of the river, the *Binnenalster Door* also recalls the *Overture Chair* from 1972, which was similarly surrounded by water. While immense in relation to human scale, when viewed from the banks of the river, it regains its intimate proportions. A door usually serves to provide access through some barrier wall, but like a "gate in a field with no fence" the *Binnenalster Door* becomes a metaphorical reference to passages in space and time, a kind of monument to the past and future, to memory. A smaller version several meters high was constructed and concurrently presented in the exhibition *Mediale,* in Hamburg (Feb–March, 1993), for which Wilson also designed the spaces for the technical and commercial portion of the exhibition.

During the creation of MR BOJANGLES in 1991, Wilson was invited by the Boymans-van Beuningen Museum in Rotterdam to serve as a guest curator for an exhibition two years hence. The exhibition would be the third of a special series of biannual presentations of its permanent collection. Harald Szeemann, the contemporary art historian, had served in this capacity in 1989, and Peter Greenaway, the filmmaker, in 1991. Here, Wilson was confronted with the challenge of creating an exhibition comprised solely of works by other artists. Wilson's contribution would be the selection and arrangement of works. He applied a three-part structure as he had many times before and returned to the theme of "portrait/still life/landscape" that he had explored briefly in the 1976 video installation, *Spaceman.* Wilson titled the exhibition *Portrait/Still Life/Landscape* (May 16 – July 11, 1993). These forms were not categorical descriptions of works on view, but metaphorical references to the body: portrait as the feet was experienced first; still life as the torso was experienced next; and landscape as the head was experienced last. Piet de Jong, curator of the Museum, explained the exhibition's structure:

> The first gallery—the lightest and fullest—is the ground, the feet…. The lighting is neutral.
> In the large [second] gallery he has created ten rooms, each supposed to contain one object and one painting…. The ten rooms are the torso of the exhibition. [Wilson] sometimes refers to them as the "ribs." The lighting is theatrical.

Memory/Loss, 1993. Installation view. Venice Biennale.

The last gallery is an empty, very wide space. The viewer is to be blinded by light.... This room is the exhibition's head....
He calls this room the head because it generates the experience of something intangible and mysterious.[6]

We are reminded by his design of this exhibition that Wilson's creative work is not a quest for mastery of one or another or all crafts, nor is it a search for the right way to express one or many of his ideas. Instead, it is the application of a process of thinking that leads *us*, not him, to a heightened awareness of things around us, of the essential humanness of what we do, of the mysterious and human capacity to learn.

Memory/Loss was created for the 1993 Venice Biennale. Wilson describes the work as an architectural poem of sculpture, sound, and light. It was inspired by a letter written to Wilson in 1987 by the German playwright Heiner Müller:

> ... A text by Tshinghis Aitmatov describes a Mongolian torture which served to turn captives into slaves, tools without memory. The technology was simple: the captive, who had been sentenced to survival and not designated for the slave trade but for domestic use by the conquerors, had his head shaved and covered with a helmet made from the skin of a freshly slaughtered camel's neck. The captive was buried to the shoulders, and exposed to the sun on the steppe, which dried the helmet and contracted it around the skull so the regrowing hair was forced to grow back into the scalp. The tortured prisoner lost his memory within five days, if he survived, and was, after this operation, a laborer who didn't cause trouble, a "Mankurt." ... There is no revolution without memory.[7]

Wilson manifested this compelling image in a cavernous, brick-walled space lighted to dramatize its scale and vacantness. In the midst of a sea of cracked, dried earth, the bust of a man could be seen with the skin helmet as described in Müller's letter. By emphasizing the vast horizontal wasteland, Wilson portrays the loss of time, the loss of memory. He said at that time, "Thinking about Venice, most of what we see here is a reflection of the past, of death. Memory loss: I like the word loss. It's short, precise, and it has many meanings."[8] For this work, Wilson received the Biennale's Golden Lion award for sculpture. The award caused a controversy among those who still do not accept Wilson as a real artist.

Three Rooms, presented at the Akira Ikeda Gallery in New York in 1994, was a trilogy of spaces based on the four elements of earth, air, wind and fire. While never stated, *Three Rooms* also seemed to be a visual essay on the spiritual choice between heaven and hell. The smallest and pivotal room was based on Rembrandt's painting of 1635, *The Offering of Abraham. In* this small, deep-green room, cast-wax hands and a dagger were suspended over a cracked mud floor, together symbolizing God's deadly demand that Abraham sacrifice his son to prove his love and obedience to God's word. On either side of this room, two other rooms offered prospective visions of the outcome of Abraham's decision: one was a bright, white dream space; the other a darkly glowing, prison-like chamber. The dark room was drawn from images developed in *Death, Destruction and Detroit,* including the Rudolf Hess Beach Chairs, oversized, red-glowing glass light bulbs, and out-of-focus photographic images of Rudolf Hess indolently raking leaves in the yard of Spandau Prison. The light room was arrestingly white and almost painfully bright. The floor was covered in a white fiber filling, a golden ladder led upwards toward the ceiling, and seemingly weightless objects sat on the floor and floated in the air. Throughout the spaces, music, sound, and text environments created by Scott Lehrer reinforced Wilson's symbolism.

The immense subterranean vaults of London's former prison, the Clink, were the site of a sprawling series of tableaux titled *H. G.,* created in the fall of 1995 by Wilson in collaboration with Hans Peter Kuhn and Michael Howells, an art director who has also worked with filmmaker Peter Greenaway. This was an unabashedly theatrical orchestration of space, light, decoration, and visual effects operating in the mode of (and flirting with the cliché of) a carnival haunted house.

The "H. G." of the work's title is H. G. Wells, whose novel, *The Time Machine,* had been published in London one hundred years before. In the opening scene, a comfortable, after-dinner conversation, Wells's character concludes that time is the fourth dimension of space, and that we move constantly through time into memory and imagination. The following is a highly excerpted journey through the installation as described by Richard Dorment:

> Entering from the street through a door with a brass plaque engraved with the initials "H. G.," we find ourselves in a luxurious Victorian dining room. The host and his guests have just risen from what was a highly enjoyable dinner party. The beeswax candles haven't yet burned out, food is still on the plates … and an unseen clock is loudly ticking. On a side-table lies a copy of *The Times* dated 1895, the year Wells published his classic of science fiction.… Like the book's opening chapter, the dining room is merely a prologue to our real journey, which begins as we descend a staircase into the medieval vaults below.… At first, cavernous spaces rhythmically illuminated by a sweeping searchlight … sounds of trickling water and squeaking rats.… A single note is struck on a far-off piano.

Three Rooms, 1994. Installation for the *Hess Room*. Akira Ikeda Gallery, New York.

H. G., 1995. Installation views. The Clink Street Vaults, London.

Watermill Center, 1996. Watermill, New York.

Over there, a swirl of fog is pierced by a shaft of brilliant sunlight falling on a mummified corpse. Across the way stands a shadowy figure, lit from behind and wearing a Victorian greatcoat, glid[ing] with infinitesimal slowness towards us.

An infirmary. Amid dozens of immaculately made-up hospital beds, we are appalled to discover buckets of blood.... We have moved forward in time. The papers chart the numbers of deaths in the influenza epidemic of 1919.... An old wireless is broadcasting German propaganda.

The connecting thread through all this is our unseen host, H. G. We come across his watch, hip flask and scent bottle ... seventeenth-century framed portraits, Egyptian excavations and a full-scaled classical colonnade [with a hundred arrows suspended in a fusillade overhead.] ... The scary whistling and plunking piano gives way to full orchestras playing swelling elegies. [9]

Architecture

More and more, Wilson has turned his energies to the architectural manipulation of space, the experiences of time, and the accumulated memories that people acquire as they encounter his constructions. It is only natural that he would turn his attention to the design and creation of self-standing structures as he is doing on eastern Long Island, New York state, in the village of Water Mill.

The Watermill Center embodies Wilson's vision for a center of aesthetic study, practice, and creation that started in the Spring Street loft in the 1960s. In 1971, he purchased land in a remote part of British Columbia where he had hoped to establish a secluded theater center. Its utter isolation worked against his plan and he abandoned it a few years later. At that time, though, he visited Water Mill (one of the several villages on eastern Long Island that comprise "The Hamptons") and created small works in collaboration with Kenneth King, Jerome Robbins, and The Byrds. Over the years, Wilson returned often at the invitation of friends with large summer houses, to work in relative calm on new pieces. Finally, in the late 1980s, he found a large, vacant, secluded industrial building that could suit his long-held vision. In 1992, he established the Watermill Center and began renovation of the unique site.

Constructed originally as the research laboratory of the Western Union Telegraph Company, the building was enlarged over the years and, in 1947, was the site where the technology for the fax machine was invented. Its location and history conspired to make this an ideal setting for Wilson to create his own works and support the works of other artists through short- and long-term residencies. It will also eventually house his extensive archives and collections of theatrical and artistic objects, and the collections of art and artifacts that he has assembled during his travels.

The configuration of the original building will be maintained while all its facilities are modernized. Small work spaces and large theater studios will replace cramped laboratories. Sleeping quarters and cooking facilities along with a large dining room will provide a communal environment for residents. Existing outbuildings will be relocated and restored, and a new structure is envisioned adjacent to the main building, to be used for exhibitions and meetings.

Since the mid- to late-1980s, Wilson has turned his creative energy more and more to tangible objects and the design of space and, at Watermill, the creation of useful architecture. The Watermill Center is still a laboratory, but now it is devoted to artistic creation and research. The design for its renovation embodies Wilson's philosophy that everything around us informs the work we do. Its austere proportions and economical materials draw considerable inspiration from the teachings of Walter Gropius and the lessons of the Bauhaus School. During occasional, informal lectorials around the dinner table, Wilson comfortably takes on the role of teacher, guiding architecture students and assembled dancers, composers, writers, and interested friends through his vision of a world where art is consistent with life and where attention to details leads to a clearer grasp of the big picture.

In Wilson's mind, the Watermill Center will never be finished. It will always a center for learning and expanding possibilities. It will always be like the subtitle for the performance *KA MOUNTAIN...* : "a story about a family and some people changing." Recalling his own educational experience, Wilson writes:

> From a small town in Texas I came to New York City. I went to the Pratt Institute. There were no planned lectures or instruction. One saw slide presentations in the lectures of Sibyll Moholy-Nagy. She taught the history of architecture. There were different kinds of energies. A Byzantine mosaic to a prehistoric Sumarian pot to a 1922 telephone. We were bombarded by different kinds of visual information. In the lecture, the verbal information was something else. So what we heard was not what we saw. And we had to freely associate with what we were seeing and what we were hearing. Not necessarily as a collage but as a construction. And then one would have an examination. And one was asked very specific information. And students were perturbed and disturbed because we had not been given the answers. The process of learning was much longer than one semester or five semesters or a five-year course. It was a way of thinking, a lifetime experience of associations. [10]

Notes

[1] L. Shyer, *Robert Wilson and his Collaborators*, 291–293.

[2] Owens, "Robert Wilson: Tableaux," *Art in America*, Nov. 1980, 114.

[3] T. Fairbrother, *Robert Wilson's Vision*, 36.

[4] CNAM, press package, 3–4.

[5] from comments in interview with Thierry Grillet in CNAM exhibition press package, 8.

[6] P. de Jong, *Memory of a Revolution*, exhibition catalogue, n.p.

[7] letter from Heiner Müller to Robert Wilson, 1987, quoted in Venice Biennale exhibition visitor's handout.

[8] "Robert Wilson: Memory Loss," *Flash Art Daily*, June 10, 1993, n.p.

[9] Richard Dorment, "Doing Time in the Clink," *The (London) Daily Telegraph*, September 13, 1995, 18.

[10] Robert Wilson in *Portrait, Still Life, Landscape*, 1993, n.p.

THEATER

1964

Dance Event at New York World's Fair. New York

Dance Pieces at Peerless Movie House. New York

Junk Dances, by Murray Louis. New York

Landscapes, by Murray Louis. New York

1965

Duricglte & Tomorrow, by Robert Wilson; music by Praetorius. New York

America Hurrah, by Jean-Claude van Itallie. New York

Modern Dance, by Robert Wilson. Waco, TX

Silent Play, performed by Robert Wilson et al. San Antonio, TX

1966

Clorox and Opus 2 (ballet). New York

1967

Baby Blood [an Evening with Baby Byrd Johnson and Baby Blood], performed by Robert Wilson. New York

1968

Alley Cats, duet with Meredith Monk. New York

BYRDwoMAN, performed by Robert Wilson, S. K. Dunn, Kikuo Saito, Raymond Andrews, Hope Kondrat, Robyn Brentano, Meredith Monk et al. New York

Theatre Activity, 1 and 2, performed by Robert Wilson, Kenneth King et al. New York

1969

The King of Spain, by Byrd Hoffman (Robert Wilson), performed by Robert Wilson and the Byrd Hoffman School of Byrds. New York

The Life and Times of Sigmund Freud, by Robert Wilson, performed by Robert Wilson and the Byrd Hoffman School of Byrds. New York

1970

Handbill, by Robert Wilson; texts by Kenneth King; music by Alan Lloyd and Julie Weber; performed by Robert Wilson et al. Iowa City, IA

Deafman Glance, by Robert Wilson; music by Alan Lloyd, Igor Weber et al; performed by Robert Wilson, Raymond Andrews, Sheryl Sutton et al. Iowa City, IA; New York; Nancy; Rome; Paris; Amsterdam

1971

Watermill (performance), music by Melvin Andringa, Igor Demjen, Alan Lloyd, Pierre Luiz; performed by Robert Wilson, Andrew de Groat, Cindy Lubar et al. Morristown, NJ

Program Prologue Now: Overture for a Deafman, by Robert Wilson. Paris

1972

Overture [New York (overture for KA MOUNTAIN AND GUARDenia TERRACE)], performed by Robert Wilson and the Byrd Hoffman School of Byrds. New York

Overture [Shiraz (overture for KA MOUNTAIN AND GUARDenia TERRACE)], performed by Robert Wilson and the Byrd Hoffman School of Byrds. Shiraz, Iran

KA MOUNTAIN AND GUARDenia TERRACE: a story about a family and some people changing, directed by Robert Wilson, Andrew de Groat, Cindy Lubar, James Neu, Ann Wilson, Mel Andringa, S. K. Dunn et al, texts by Robert Wilson, Andrew de Groat, Jessie Dunn Gilbert, Kikuo Saito, Cindy Lubar, Susan Sheehy, and Ann Wilson; music by Igor Demjen; performed by Robert Wilson and the Byrd Hoffman School of Byrds. Shiraz, Iran

Overture [Paris (overture for KA MOUNTAIN AND GUARDenia TERRACE)], by Robert Wilson, Melvin Andringa, Kathryn Kean, Kikuo Saito, Ann Wilson et al; music by Igor Demjen; performed by Robert Wilson and the Byrd Hoffman School of Byrds. Paris

1973

King Lyre and Lady in the Wasteland, performed by Robert Wilson and Elaine Luthy. New York

The Life and Times of Joseph Stalin, by Robert Wilson; music by Alan Lloyd, Igor Demjen, Julie Weber, Michael Galasso; texts by Robert Wilson, Cindy Lubar, Christopher Knowles, Ann Wilson. Performed by Robert Wilson and the Byrd Hoffman School of Byrds. Copenhagen; New York; São Paulo

1974

DiaLog / A Mad Man A Mad Giant A Mad Dog A Mad Urge A Mad Face, by Robert Wilson and Christopher Knowles; performed by Robert Wilson, Christopher Knowles et al. Rome; Washington D.C.; Shiraz, Iran; Milan

Prologue to A Letter for Queen Victoria, by Robert Wilson; music by Kathryn Cation and Michael Galasso. Spoleto, Italy

A Letter for Queen Victoria, by Robert Wilson. Additional texts by Christopher Knowles, Cindy Lubar, Stefan Brecht, James Neu. Spoleto, Italy; La Rochelle, France; Belgrade; Paris; Zurich; Thonon-les Bains, Sochaux-Doubs, Mulhouse, Lyon, and Nice, France; New York

1975

A Solo Reading, voice and drawings by Robert Wilson; music by Alan Lloyd. New York

The $ Value of Man, by Robert Wilson and Christopher Knowles; music by Michael Galasso. New York

DiaLog [2], by Robert Wilson and Christopher Knowles; performed by Robert Wilson and Christopher Knowles. New London, CT; New York

To Street: One Man Show, performed by Robert Wilson. Bonn

1976

reconfirmation of reservations, Robert Wilson solo. Milan; Brescia, Italy

Bob Wilson solo [including excerpts from *Deafman Glance, A Letter for Queen Victoria,* and *The King of Spain*]. Rennes, France; Hamburg; Rotterdam; Capri

Einstein on the Beach, by Robert Wilson and Philip Glass; music by Philip Glass; texts by Christopher Knowles, Samuel M. Johnson, and Lucinda Childs. New York; Avignon, France; Venice; Belgrade; Brussels; Paris; Hamburg; Rotterdam; Amsterdam

DiaLog [3], by Robert Wilson and Christopher Knowles; performed by Robert Wilson, Christopher Knowles, and Lucinda Childs. New York; New Brunswick, NJ; Washington, D.C.

1977

DiaLog / Network, by Robert Wilson and Christopher Knowles; texts by Christopher

Knowles. Florence; Munich; Paris; Boston; Amsterdam; Minneapolis; Chicago; Brussels
I Was Sitting On My Patio This Guy Appeared I Thought I Was Hallucinating, by Robert Wilson, codirected by Lucinda Childs; music by Alan Lloyd. Ypsilanti, MI; Philadelphia; Austin, Clear Lake, Forth Worth, TX; Los Angeles; San Francisco; St. Paul, MN; New York; Paris; Rotterdam, Den Hague, and Amsterdam, Netherlands; Zurich; Geneva; Milan; Berlin; Stuttgart; London

1979

Death Destruction and Detroit: a Play with Music in 2 Acts / a Love Story in 16 Scenes, by Robert Wilson; music by Alan Lloyd, Keith Jarrett, Randy Newman. Berlin
Edison, by Robert Wilson; music by Michael Riesman et al. New York; Villeurbanne, France; Milan; Paris

1980

Overture to the Fourth Act of Deafman Glance, by Robert Wilson. Brussels and Liège, Belgium; Montréal
DiaLog / Curious George, by Robert Wilson and Christopher Knowles, texts by Christopher Knowles. Turin; Warsaw; Rotterdam; New York

1981

The Man in the Raincoat, by Robert Wilson, performed by Robert Wilson, music by Hans Peter Kuhn. Cologne
The CIVIL warS: a Tree is Best Measured When it is Down, first workshop. Munich
Relative Calm, by Lucinda Childs; lights and design by Robert Wilson; music by John Gibson. Strasbourg; Bordeaux; Nice; Grenoble; New York

1982

Die Goldenen Fenster, by Robert Wilson (German version); music by Tania Léon, Gavin Bryars, and Johann Pepusch. Munich, Vienna
Great Day in the Morning, by Robert Wilson and Jessye Norman; music by Jessye Norman and Charles Lloyd Jr. Paris
Overture to the Fourth Act of Deafman Glance, by Robert Wilson; performed by Robert Wilson, Carol Miles, and Chizuko Sugiura. Fribourg, Switzerland; Toga-mura, Japan

1983

The CIVIL warS: a Tree is Best Measured When it is Down [act I, scene B], by Robert Wilson; music by Nicolas Economou. Rotterdam; Paris; Nîmes; Grenoble; Lyon; Nice; Bordeaux; Lille; Le Havre

1984

The Knee Plays [from *the CIVIL warS*], by Robert Wilson and David Byrne; music and texts by David Byrne. Minneapolis, MN; Frankfurt; Paris; Madrid; Venice; Bologne; Cologne; Cambridge, MA; Los Angeles; Berkeley; Boulder, CO; Albuquerque, NM; Iowa City, IA; Detroit; Washington, D.C.; New York; Burlington, VT; Watermill; Austin, Houston, TX; Chicago; Tokyo; Brisbane, Australia
The CIVIL warS: a Tree is Best Measured When it is Down [act I, scene A; act III, scene E; act IV, scene A; epilogue], by Robert Wilson and Heiner Müller; music by Philip Glass, David Byrne, Hans Peter Kuhn, Frederick the Great, Thomas Tallis, Franz Schubert. Cologne; Berlin; Cambridge, MA
The CIVIL warS: a Tree is Best Measured When it is Down [prologue; act V], by Robert Wilson and Philip Glassl; music by Philip Glass; texts by Maita di Niscemi. Rome; Los Angeles; Scheveningen, Utrecht, Eindhoven, and Amsterdam, Netherlands; New York
The CIVIL warS: a Tree is Best Measured When it is Down [act II, scenes A and B; act III, scenes A and B]. Marseille
The CIVIL warS: a Tree is Best Measured When it is Down [act I, scene C; act II, scene C; act III, scenes C and D]. Tokyo
Médée, by Marc-Antoine Charpentier; texts by Thomas Corneille. Lyon
Medea, based on Euripides's text; texts by Robert Wilson and Gavin Bryars, Heiner Müller and Vladimir Majakowskij; music by Gavin Bryars. Lyon; Paris

1985

King Lear, by William Shakespeare; music by Daniel Birnbaum. Los Angeles
Reading/Performance 1969–1984, texts by Robert Wilson, Christopher Knowles, Ben Halley, Chris Moore, and David Byrne; performed by Robert Wilson. Dublin; Ghent; Cambridge, MA

The Golden Windows, by Robert Wilson (U.S. version). New York

1986

Alcestis, based on Euripides's text; adapted by Robert Wilson; translated by Dudley Fitts and Robert Fitzgerald; texts by Heiner Müller; music by Hans Peter Kuhn and Laurie Anderson. Cambridge, MA; Paris
Hamletmaschine, by Heiner Müller (U.S. version), translated by Carl Weber; music by Jerry Leiber and Mike Stoller. New York; Nanterre, France; Madrid; Saint Etienne and Lille, France; London; Nice; Palermo. German version: Hamburg; Berlin
Alceste, by Christoph Willibald Gluck, based on Euripides's text. Stuttgart

1987

Parzival: Auf der anderen Seite des Sees, by Robert Wilson and Tankred Dorst; texts by Tankred Drost and Christopher Knowles; music by Tassilo Jelde. Hamburg
Quartett, adapted from *Les Liaisons Dangereuses* by Chodelors de Laclos; texts by Heiner Müller (German version); music by Christoph Eschenbach. Stuttgart
Overture to the Fourth Act of Deafman Glance, by Robert Wilson; performed by Robert Wilson and Sheryl Sutton. Delphi, Greece; New York
The Man in the Raincoat, by Robert Wilson; music by Laurie Anderson; directed by Rob Malasch; performed by Michael Matthews. Amsterdam
Alkestis based on Euripides's text (German version), translated by Friederike Roth and Ann-Christin Rommen. Stuttgart
Death, Destruction & Detroit II, texts by Franz Kafka, Heiner Müller, Robert Wilson, Maita di Niscemi, Cindy Lubar; music by Hans Peter Kuhn. Berlin
Salomé, by Richard Strauss, adapted from Oscar Wilde's text. Milan

1988

The Forest, texts by Heiner Müller and Darryl Pickney; music by David Byrne. Berlin; Munich; New York
Cosmopolitan Greetings, texts by Allen Ginsberg; music by Rolf Liebermann and George Gruntz. Hamburg

Le Martyre de Saint Sébastien, texts by Gabriele D'Annunzio; music by Claude Debussy; choreography by Robert Wilson and Suzushi Hanayagi. Paris; New York
Quartet (U.S. version), music by Martin Pearlman. Cambridge, MA

1989

Swan Song, by Anton Chekov. Munich; Tokyo
Orlando, based on the novel by Virginia Woolf; adapted by Robert Wilson and Darryl Pinkney; music by Hans Peter Kuhn; German version performed by Jutta Lampe. Berlin
la Nuit d'Avant le Jour, opening of Opéra Bastille; music by Gounod, Mayerbeer, Massenet, Gluck, Saint Saëns, Bizet, and Berlioz
Die Materie, by Robert Wilson; music by Louis Andressen. Amsterdam and Den Hague, Netherlands
Doktor Faustus, based on the novel by Thomas Mann; music by Giacomo Manzoni. Milan

1990

What Room: A Play for 3 Minutes, by Robert Wilson. Cambridge, MA
The Black Rider: The Casting of the Magic Bullets, texts by August Apfel, Friedrich Laun, and Thomas de Quincey; adapted by Robert Wilson; texts by William S. Burroughs; music by Tom Waits. Thalia Theater, Hamburg; Vienna; Paris; Amsterdam; Berlin; Genoa; Seville; New York; Dortmund, Heilbronn, Weimar, and Wiesbaden, Germany
King Lear, by William Shakespeare. Frankfurt

1991

The Malady of Death, by Marguerite Duras; music by Hans Peter Kuhn. Schaubühne am Lehniner Platz, Berlin
Grace for Grace, by Robert Wilson. New York
Lohengrin, by Richard Wagner. Zurich
The Magic Flute, by Wolfgang Amadeus Mozart. Opéra Bastille, Paris
Parsifal, by Richard Wagner. Hamburg; Houston, TX
When we Dead Awaken, by Henrik Ibsen; English version by Robert Brustein; adapted by Robert Wilson; music by Charles "Honi" Coles. Cambridge, MA; Houston, TX; São Paulo

1992

Alice, based on *Alice in Wonderland* by Lewis Carroll; texts by Paul Schmidt; music by Tom Waits. Hamburg and Ludwigshaven, Germany; Lisbon
Danton's Death, by Georg Büchner; English version by Robert Auletta. Houston, TX
Don Juan Último, by Vincente Molina Foix; music by Mariano Diaz. Madrid
Dr. Faustus Lights the Lights, by Gertrude Stein; music by Hans Peter Kuhn. Berlin; Frankfurt; Venice; Rome; New York; Salzburg; Maubeuge; Paris; Antwerp; Milan; Montreal; Edinburgh; Lisbon; Budapest; Prague; Hong Kong

1993

Madame Butterfly, by Giacomo Puccini. Opéra Bastille, Paris
Alice in Bed, by Susan Sontag; music by Hans Peter Kuhn. Berlin
Orlando, French version performed by Isabelle Huppert. Théâtre Vidy, Lausanne; Paris; Milan; Strasbourg; Brest, France; Lisbon; Nîmes; Brussels; Rennes, France
Orlando, Danish version performed by Susse Wold. Betty Nansen Teatret, Copenhagen

1994

Der Mond im Gras: einmal keinmal immer, based on stories by the Brothers Grimm and Georg Büchner; music by Robert Schulkowsky. Münchner Kammerspiele, Munich
Hanjo/Hagoromo: Dittico Giapponese, by Yukio Mishima and Zeami; music and libretto by Marcello Panni and Jo Kondo. Teatro della Pergola, Florence; Lille, France
T.S.E.: "Come in Under the Shadow of this Red Rock," by Robert Wilson; music by Philip Glass. Wiemar; Gibellina, Sicily
The Meek Girl, based on a story by F. Dostoyevski; adapted by Robert Wilson and Wolfgang Wiens; music by Stephan Kurt and Gerd Bessler; performed by Robert Wilson, Charles Chemin, Louis Ardeal, Marianna Kavallieratos, Thomas Lehmann. Festival d'Automne, Paris; Antwerp; Zurich; Grenoble; Frankfurt; Caen, France
Skin, Meat, Bone: The Wesleyan Project, by Robert Wilson and Alvin Lucien; music by Alvin Lucien. Middletown, CT

1995

Snow on the Mesa, the Martha Graham Dance Company. Washington; New York; Paris; Amsterdam; Pittsburgh, PA
Bluebeard's Castle/Erwartung, by Bela Bartok and Arnold Schönberg. Opera Zurich (*Bluebeard's Castle* only, paired with *Oedipus Rex*); Salzburg
Persephone, texts by Brad Gooch based on the poetry of Ovid; music by Philip Glass. New York; Delphi, Greece; Istanbul
HAMLET: A Monologue, by William Shakespeare; adapted by Robert Wilson and Wolfgang Wiens; music by Hans Peter Kuhn. Houston, TX; Venice; Lincoln, NE; Paris; Seville; Lisbon; Helsinki; Vienna
Knee Plays and Other Acts: A Gala Benefit for the Kitchen (version of *Skin, Meat, ...,* 1994), by Robert Wilson and Alvin Lucien; music by Alvin Lucien. New York

1996

Oedipus Rex, (paired with *Bluebeard's Castle,* 1995). Opera Zurich; Paris
Orlando, based on the novel by Virginia Woolf; English version performed by Miranda Richardson. Edinburgh Festival
Time Rocker, texts by Darryl Pinckney; music by Lou Reed. Thalia Theater, Hamburg
Four Saints in three Acts, music by Virgil Thomson; texts by Gertrude Stein. Edinburgh Festival; Houston, TX; New York

FILM AND VIDEO

1963

Slant, by Robert Wilson, for WNET-TV

1965

The House (unfinished), performed by Jearnine Wagner

1970

Watermill (16mm)

1971

Overture for a Deafman (16mm)

1976

The Spaceman (video performance), by

Robert Wilson and Ralph Hilton; performed by Robert Wilson, Ralph Hilton, Christopher Knowles, Sue Sheehy et al

1978
Video 50, by Robert Wilson; directed by Robert Wilson; music by Alan Lloyd; performed by Robert Wilson et al. Produced by Film/Video Collectif, Lausanne, in association with Zweites Deutsches Fernsehen

1981
Deafman Glance [also: *The Murder*], by Robert Wilson; directed by Robert Wilson. Produced by Louis Bianchi and Byrd Hoffman Foundation for the Corporation for Public Broadcasting.

1982
Stations, by Robert Wilson; directed by Robert Wilson; music by Jacob Stern and Nicolas Economou; choreography by Jim Self. Produced by Byrd Hoffman Foundation, Zweites Deutsches Fernsehen, and Institut National de l'Audiovisuel

1984
The Spaceman (video installation), by Robert Wilson and Ralph Hilton

1989
The Death of King Lear. Produced by Television Española
La Femme à la Cafetière, after a painting by Paul Cézanne. Co-produced by Musée d'Orsay, Institut National de l'Audiovisuel, and La Sept

1991
Mr. Bojangle's Memory. Produced by CCI/Centre Georges Pompidou

1992
Don Juan Último, texts by Vincente Molina Foix. Produced by Telemadrid and Centro Dramatico Nacional

1994
The Tragedy of Hamlet, Prince of Denmark, by Richard Rutkowski; based on the play by Shakespeare; performed by Heiko Senst, Robert Wilson et al. Produced by See-No-

Evil Productions, New York. Filmed at Watermill Center, Long Island, New York
The Death of Molière [La Mort de Molière], a film on video by Robert Wilson; scenario by Robert Wilson, Philippe Chemin, and Jan Linders, texts by Heiner Müller et al; music by Philip Glass. Produced by La Sept/ARTE and Institut National de l'Audiovisuel

SOLO EXHIBITIONS AND MUSEUM INSTALLATIONS

1967
Poles (outdoor sculpture). Grail Retreat, Loveland, OH

1971
Willard Gallery, New York

1974
Robert Wilson: Dessins et Sculptures. Musée Galliera, Paris

1975
Galerie Wunsche, Berlin

1976
Robert Wilson: Sculpture & Drawings. Iolas Gallery-Brooks Jackson Inc., New York

1977
Robert Wilson: Furniture/Multiples. Marian Goodman Gallery, New York

1978
Robert Wilson: Skulpturen. Galerie Folker Skulima, Berlin

1979
Marian Goodman Gallery, New York
Galerie Folker Skulima, Berlin
Galerie Zwirner, Cologne
Paula Cooper Gallery, New York

1980
Robert Wilson / From a Theatre of Images. The Contemporary Arts Center, Cincinnati, OH

1982
Drawings for the Golden Windows. Marian

Goodman Gallery, New York
Robert Wilson: dessins pour "Medea" / "Great Day in the Morning." Galerie le Dessin, Paris
Robert Wilson: The Golden Windows/Die Goldenen Fenster: Die Zeichungen. Galerie Annemarie Verna, Zurich
Franz Morat Institut, Fribourg, Switzerland

1983
Robert Wilson: Dessins pour "the CIVIL warS." Pavillion des Arts, Paris
Robert Wilson: "Civil Wars." Galerie Brinkman, Amsterdam
Boymans-van Beuningen Museum, Rotterdam
Raum für Kunst, Produzentaengalerie, Hamburg
Festival Mondial du Théâtre, Nancy, France
Robert Wilson: Drawings. Gallery Ueda, Tokyo
Sogetsu School, Tokyo
Drawings from the CIVIL warS. Leo Castelli, Richard L. Feigen, James Corcoran; New York
Works by Robert Wilson. Museum of Art, Rhode Island School of Design, Providence, RI

1984
Robert Wilson: Drawings. Paula Cooper Gallery, New York
Robert Wilson's the CIVIL warS: a tree is best measured when it is down: Drawings, Models, and World Wide Documentation. Exhibition Center, Otis Art Institute, Los Angeles
Robert Wilson: drawings for the CIVIL warS: a tree is best measured when it is down: and Selected Videos. Jones Troyer Gallery, Washington, D.C.
Robert Wilson: Dessins Pour Trois Operas: Medea 1981, Great Day in the Morning 1982, Civil Wars 1984. ARCA (Centre d'Art Contemporain), Marseille
Robert Wilson: Zeichnungen und Skulpturen. Kölnischer Kunstverein, Cologne
Walker Art Center, Minneapolis, MN
Museo del Folklore, Rome

1985
Robert Wilson: Medea e Parsifal: Disegni, Incisioni, Video. Galleria Franca Mancini, Pesaro, Italy
Parsifal Lithographs. Werkraum der Münchner Kammerspiele, Munich

1986

Robert Wilson: Drawings. University of Iowa, Iowa City
The Knee Plays: Drawings. KiMo Gallery, Albuquerque, NM
Hamletmaschine: Drawings. Theater in der Kunsthalle, Hamburg
Robert Wilson: Drawings for the Stage (retrospective exhibit). Laguna Gloria Museum, Austin, TX
Hamletmaschine: Drawings. Grey Art Gallery, New York University, New York
Drawings: the CIVIL warS: Robert Wilson. Hewlett Gallery, Carnegie-Mellon University, Pittsburgh, PA
Robert Wilson: Transmutation of Archetypes: Medea & Parsifal (traveling exhibition). Lehman College Art Gallery, City University of New York; Hewlett Gallery, Carnegie-Mellon University, Pittsburgh, PA; Kuhlenschmidt Gallery, Los Angeles
Robert Wilson: The Complete "Parsifal" Portfolio: Drawings for Theatre Pieces. The Alpha Gallery, Boston
Robert Wilson: Drawings: Alcestis. The Harcus Gallery, Boston
Robert Wilson: Drawings for "the CIVIL warS." Rhona Hoffman Gallery, Chicago

1987

Robert Wilson: die lithographischen Zyklen, 1984–1986: Medea, Parsifal, Alceste. Galerie Fred Jahn, Munich; Galerie im Theater der Stadt Gütersloh
Robert Wilson: "Parzival." Galerie Harald Behm, Hamburg
Drawings. Galerie Biedermann, Munich
Robert Wilson: Erinnerung an eine Revolution. Kunstgebäude am Schloßplatz, Galerie der Stadt, Stuttgart
Robert Wilson: Drawings, Furniture and Props for "Alceste," "Alcestis," "the CIVIL warS," "Death, Destruction & Detroit II," "Hamletmaschine," "Salome." Paula Cooper Gallery, New York; Aldrich Museum of Contemporary Art, Ridgefield, CT

1988

Dreams and Images: The Theater of Robert Wilson. Rare Book and Manuscript Library, Butler Library, Columbia University, New York

Drawings. Marlene Eleini Gallery, London
Robert Wilson: die lithographischen Zyklen, 1984–1986: Medea, Parsifal, Alceste. Galerie Fred Jahn, Munich
Cosmopolitan Greetings. Galerie Harald Behm, Hamburg

1989

Swan Song (disegni). Galerie Fred Jahn, Munich
Robert Wilson: Orlando: 22 Drawings and Furniture. Annemarie Verna Galerie, Zurich
Robert Wilson: La Nuit d'avant le jour: Dessins. Yvon Lambert, Paris
Erinnerung an eine Revolution. Galerie Fabian Walter, Basel
Robert Wilson: Drawings for the Opera 'Die Materie' by Louis Andriessen. Stedelijk Museum, Amsterdam
Robert Wilson: Zeichnungen und Druckgrafik. Galerie Lüpcke, Frankfurt
Robert Wilson: die lithographischen Zyklen 1984–1986. Museum Morsbroich, Leverkusen, Germany

1990

Robert Wilson: Alceste Drawings and Furniture/Sculpture. Feigen Incorporated, Chicago
Robert Wilson: Drawings, Sculpture and Furniture, "the CIVIL warS." Virginia Lynch Gallery, Tiverton, RI
King Lear. Kunsthalle Shirn, Frankfurt
Robert Wilson: Choreographie des Designs. Ambiente, Interior Design and . . . (AIDA), Hamburg

1991

Robert Wilson: Zeichnungen-Zyklen: A Letter for Queen Victoria, 1971/2: Golden Windows, 1981/2: Civil Wars, 1983: Swan Song, 1989. Galerie Fred Jahn, Munich
Robert Wilson: Monuments. Kestner-Gesellschaft, Hannover, Germany; Bayerische Akademie der Schönen Künsten, Munich
Robert Wilson: Mr. Bojangles' Memory: og son of fire. Centre Georges Pompidou, Paris
Robert Wilson: Lohengrin Drawings and Other Works. Annemarie Verna Galerie, Zurich
Robert Wilson: Chairs for Marie and Pierre Curie, Sigmund Freud, Albert Einstein, A Table for Nijnski, and Parzival Drawings. Busche Galerie, Cologne

Die wundersame Welt des Robert Wilson (video presentation of *Video 50*, *Deafman Glance* and *Stations*). Kino Arsenal, Berlin
Robert Wilson: Drawing and Sculpture. Barbara Krakow Gallery, Boston
Robert Wilson: Drawing and Sculpture. Thomas Segal Gallery, Boston
Robert Wilson: Die lithographischen Zyklen und Zeichnungen . . . Palais Stutterheim, Städtische Galerie, Erlangen, Germany
Robert Wilson's Vision (traveling retrospective exhibition). Museum of Fine Arts, Boston; Contemporary Arts Museum, Houston, TX; Museum of Modern Art, San Francisco
Robert Wilson: Sculpture, Furniture, Paintings and Drawings. Paula Cooper Gallery, New York

1992

Binnenalster Door (installation), Hamburg
Robert Wilson: Works, 1972–1992. Raum für Kunst E. V., Hamburg
La Flute Enchantée: Dessins. Galerie Thaddaeus Ropac, Paris
Objects. Produzentengalerie, Hamburg
Robert Wilson: Convidados de piedra. Sala Goya, Círculo de Bellas Artes, Madrid
Einstein on the Beach. Kamakura Gallery, Tokyo
Robert Wilson. Galeria Gamarra y Garrigues, Madrid
Robert Wilson. Istituto Valeciano de Arte Moderna, Valencia
Robert Wilson: Drawings for Alice in Wonderland. Laura Carpenter Fine Art, Santa Fe, NM
Robert Wilson: Drawings. Hiram Butler Gallery, Houston, TX
Robert Wilson: White Raven Drawings. Paula Cooper Gallery, New York

1993

Robert Wilson: Deafman Glance: A Video Installation
Photographs of Robert Wilson Productions in Germany. Goethe House, New York
Robert Wilson: Memorie della Terra Desolata, Baglio delle Case di Stefano, Gibellina Nuova (Sicily)
Monsters of Grace. Galerie Franck+Shulte, Berlin
Memory/Loss (installation at the Venice Bien-

237

nale). Objects by Robert Wilson and Tadeusz Kantor; sound score by Hans Peter Kuhn; texts by Heiner Müller. Granai delle Zitelle, Venice
Portrait, Still Life, Landscape. Curated by Robert Wilson. Boymans-van Beuningen Museum, Rotterdam
Draft Notes for a Conversation on Dante (presentation of a lithograph book). Galerie van Rijsbergen, Rotterdam
Robert Wilson. Nathalie Beeckman Fine Arts, Brussels
Robert Wilson: Furniture and Other Works. Waco Creative Art Center, Waco, TX
Mediale '93 (installation). Deichtorhallen, Hamburg

1994
Der Mond im Gras drawings. Private exhibition, Galerie Biedermann, Munich
Alice. Galeria Lu's Serpa, Lisbon
Three Rooms. Akira Ikeda Gallery, New York
Disegni by Ghibellina. Paula Cooper Gallery, New York

1995
H. G. [installation]. Clink Street Vaults, London
Robert Wilson: The Rooms of Seven Women, und Zeichnungen zu den Neuinszenierungen Blaubart/Erwartung. Karl-Böhmsall des Kleinen Festspielhauses, Salzburg
Robert Wilson. Hiram Butler Gallery, Houston
Die Zauberflöte. Galerie Thaddaeus Ropac, Salzburg

1996
Installation. Galeries Lafayette, Paris
Paula Cooper Gallery, New York

SELECTED PUBLICATIONS

1970
"The King of Spain," by Byrd Hoffmann (Robert Wilson), in William H. Hoffman ed., *New American Plays*, New York, pp. 241–272.

1977
"A Letter for Queen Victoria," in Bonnie Marranca ed., *The Theater of Images*, New York, pp. 37–109.

"Réponses," transcribed by Jacqueline Lesschaeve, in *Tel Quel*, Paris, 71/73, pp. 217–225.

1978
From "Working Notes for Death, Destruction & Detroit," in *Gnome Baker II & III*, New York.

1979
"I was sitting on my patio this guy appeared I thought I was hallucinating: a play in two acts," in *Performing Arts Journal,* vol. IV:1–2, n. 10/11, pp. 200–218.

1980
"A Short Story," in Jonathan Cott and Mary Gimbel ed., *Wonders: Writings and Drawings for the Child in Us All*, New York, pp. 613–615.
(texts by Robert Wilson), in Richard Kostelanetz ed., *Text-Sound Texts*, New York, p. 321.

1984
the CIVIL warS: a tree is best measured when it is down, exhibition catalogue, Los Angeles.

1985
"Robert Wilson's Works, 1969 to 1984," transcription of a lecture, in *Congrés Internacional de Teatre a Catalunya: Actes*, Barcelona, vol. I, pp. 241–258.

1987
"A Propos de Medea . . . ," in *Drailles*, Nîmes, n. 7/8, pp. 63–64.

1988
"Notes sur l'Ouverture du IVe acte du Regard du Sourd," in *Communications: Vidéo*, Paris, n. 48, p. 342.
"Robert Wilson: Director, Designer, Theater and Visual Artist, New York City," transcription of an interview with Dodie Kazanjian, in *Artsreview: America's Opera*, Washington, D.C., n. 5:1, pp. 57–58.

1990
"On American Theatre," in *National Forum: The Phi Kappa Phi Journal,* Baton Rouge, n. LXX:3, p. 31.
"What Room: A Play for 3 Minutes," in *Theater Week*, New York, n. 3:42, pp. 32–33.

1991
Mr. Bojangle's Memory: og son of fire, exhibition catalogue, Centre Pompidou, Paris.
"Ist die Oper am Ende?," forum with contribution by Robert Wilson, in *Bühne,* Vienna, p. 30.

1992
"A Propos de Doctor Faustus Lights the Lights," April 92, excerpt from an interview, in *Théâtre/Public* 106, pp. 54–60.
"Obscure Objects of Desire," in *Preview,* Museum of Fine Arts, Boston, p. 15.
"The Architecture of the Theatrical Space," transcription of an interview with Bettina Masuch and Tom Stromberg, in *Theaterschrift: The Written Space,* Brussels, no. 2, pp. 102–107.

1993
Notes for a Conversation on Dante, by Ossip Mandelstam, lithographs by Robert Wilson, limited edition, Picaron Ed., Amsterdam.
Portrait, Still Life, Landscape, exhibition catalogue, Boymans-van Beuningen Museum, Rotterdam.
"Works on Paper," in *Performing Arts Journal,* Baltimore, n. 43, vol. 15:1, pp. 2–22.

1994
"Momenti di Teatro: Lavoro con l'intuito. Penso che il corpo non mente mai," in *Sarad/Charade, Words and Images*, in *Dance Ink,* n. 5:1, pp. 30–35.

1995
"'Hamlet' as Autobiography, Spoken in Reflective Voice," in *The New York Times* 2 July 1995, p. H4 (transcription of an interview by Marion Kessel to Robert Wilson).
"To Place the Voice with the Face: La Juste Voix," in Georges Banu ed., *De la Parole aux Chants*, Paris, Conservatoire National Supérieur d'Art Dramatique, pp. 78–81.
"Virginia Woolf's Orlando," in *Theatre Forum: International Theatre Journal,* 6, pp. 77–87.

AWARDS

1970
Critics Award for Best Foreign Play, Le Syndicat de la Critique Musicale, Paris (*Deafman Glance*)

1971
Drama Desk Award for Direction, New York (*Deafman Glance*)

1974
OBIE Special Award Citation for Direction, New York (*The Life and Times of Joseph Stalin*)

1975
Maharam Award for Best Set Design for a Broadway Show, New York (*A Letter for Queen Victoria*)
TONY nomination for Best Score and Lyrics, New York (*A Letter for Queen Victoria*)

1977
Critics Award for Best Musical Theatre, Le Syndicat de la Critque Musicale, Paris (*Einstein on the Beach*)
Grand Prize BITEF, Belgrade (*Einstein on the Beach*)
Lumen Award for Design, New York (*Einstein on the Beach*)

1979
German Critics Award, Berlin (*Death, Destruction & Detroit*)

1982
Der Rosentrauss, Munich (*The Golden Windows*)

1984
Berlin Festspiele Theatertreffens, Cologne (*the CIVIL warS*)
First Prize, San Sebastian Film and Video Festival, San Sebastian, Spain (*Stations*)

1985
Franklin Furnace Award, New York (*Einstein on the Beach*)

1986
Nomination, Pulitzer Prize for Drama (*the CIVIL warS*)

Picasso Award, Theatre Festival, Málaga, Spain (*Overture to the Fourth Act of Deafman Glance*)
Obie Award for Direction, New York (*Hamletmaschine*)

1987
American Theatre Wing Design Award, Noteworthy Unusual Effects, New York (*the CIVIL warS*, Rome)
Bessie Award, New York
French Critics Award for Best Foreign Play, Le Syndicat de la Critique Musicale, Paris (*Alcestis*)
Berlin Festspiele Theatertreffens (*Hamletmaschine*)
Skowhegan Medal for Drawing, Skowhegan School of Painting and Sculpture, New York

1988
Institute Honor, The American Institute of Architects, New York
Premio Mondello, Award for Theatre, Palermo, Italy

1989
Gran Premio, Biennale Festival of Cinema Art, Barcelona (video: *La Femme à la Cafetière*)
Premio Abbiati, Best Production of the Year, Italian Theater Critics Award, Milan (*Dr. Faustus*)
Grand Prize for Best Event, Biennal of São Paulo (*Parzival* and *Hamletmaschine*)
Lion of the Performing Arts, Public Library, New York

1990
German Theater Critics Award, Best Production of the Year, Berlin (*The Black Rider: the casting of the magic bullets*)
Festival du Film d'Art, Special Mention by the Jury, Paris (video: *La Femme à la Cafetière*)

1991
Honorary Doctorate, Pratt Institute, New York
Jack I. and Lilian Poses for Creative Arts Award at Brandeis University, For Alternative and Multidiscipline Creative Art Forms, Waltham, MA.

1992
Premio UBU, Best Foreign Performance, Milan (*Dr. Faustus Lights the Lights*)

1993
Golden Lion Award in Sculpture, Venice Biennale (*Memory/Loss*)

1994
Premio UBU, Best Foreign Performance, Milan (*Alice*)
Honorary Doctorate, California College of Arts and Crafts, Oakland, CA

1995
Best Director, International Widescreen Festival, Amsterdam (The Death of Molière)
Premio Abbiati, Italian Theater Critics Award, Milan (*Hanjo/Hagoromo*)
Texan Artist of the Year, Art League, Houston, TX

EDUCATION

1959–1965 University of Texas, Austin, TX
1962 studied painting with George McNeil, Paris
1965 B.F.A. Architecture, Pratt Institute, Brooklyn, New York
1966 apprentice to Paolo Soleri, Arcosanti Community, Arizona

Photography Credits